Occupational Devotion

Occupational Devotion

Finding Satisfaction and Fulfillment at Work

Robert A. Stebbins

A

ANTHEM PRESS

Anthem Press
An imprint of Wimbledon Publishing Company
www.anthempress.com

This edition first published in UK and USA 2022
by ANTHEM PRESS
75–76 Blackfriars Road, London SE1 8HA, UK
or PO Box 9779, London SW19 7ZG, UK
and
244 Madison Ave #116, New York, NY 10016, USA

British Library Cataloguing-in-Publication Data
A catalogue record for this book is available from the British Library.

Library of Congress Cataloging-in-Publication Data
Names: Stebbins, Robert A., 1938– author.
Title: Occupational devotion : finding satisfaction and fulfillment at work /
Robert A. Stebbins, University of Calgary.
Description: London, UK; New York, NY : Anthem Press, an imprint of Wimbledon
Publishing Company, 2022. | Includes bibliographical references and index. |
Identifiers: LCCN 2022000094 | ISBN 9781839983139 (paperback) |
ISBN 9781839983146 (pdf) | ISBN 9781839983153 (epub)
Subjects: LCSH: Job satisfaction. | Quality of work life. | Job enrichment.
Classification: LCC HF5549.5.J63 S727 2022 |
DDC 331.01/2–dc23/eng/20220114
LC record available at https://lccn.loc.gov/2022000094

ISBN-13: 978-1-83998-313-9 (Pbk)
ISBN-10: 1-83998-313-2 (Pbk)

Cover image: Abstract pattern stripes blue watercolour textures background geo.
Watercolor geometric splash brushes digital effect overlay backdrop seamless.
Blue monochrome color lines paint and drawing. By Yulia Aksa/ Shutterstock.com

This title is also available as an e-book.

CONTENTS

List of Illustrations   vii

Preface   ix

Acknowledgments   xi

Chapter 1   Serious Pursuits   1

Chapter 2   Liberal Professions   15

Chapter 3   Consultants   31

Chapter 4   Skilled Trades and Crafts   45

Chapter 5   Small Businesses   59

Chapter 6   Conclusions   69

References   79

Index   85

ILLUSTRATIONS

Figures

1.1 The Serious Leisure Perspective   3
2.1 Serious Leisure Perspective Involvement Scale   16

Table

1.1 A Leisure-Based Theoretic Typology of Volunteers and Volunteering 4

PREFACE

Contrary to the dreary commonsense image of work, some people find it immensely appealing, even when it results in a meager living. A significant part of the explanation for this anomaly is love for the core activity of the job, such that the typical participant would do it without pay were it not for the need to make a living. Certainly, that person does not despair the resumption of work following a holiday. In other words, in this sense, all these occupational devotees are amateurs.

From this backdrop, the idea of occupational devotion, or devotee work, was conceptualized (Stebbins 2004/2014) and incorporated later in the serious leisure perspective as one of the two serious pursuits (Stebbins 2012). The other pursuit is serious leisure itself, with both forms being anchored in activities that are immensely appealing and fulfilling. Despite such desirable qualities the serious pursuits constitute a minority of all work and leisure activities, these two domains being dominated by disagreeable work and hedonic casual leisure activities.

The devotee occupations serve as full-time or part-time livelihoods for people fortunate enough to have found them. Such work has so far been observed to exist in four sectors of the economy: the liberal professions, consulting occupations, skilled trades and small business proprietors. In ways to be set out in the coming chapters, devotee work roots in serious leisure, and many participants in the latter have no desire to pursue the former. Moreover, some of those who do "quit their day job" to try to make a living at their leisure passion fail to achieve this dream and are forced to return to pure amateur, hobbyist or career volunteer status. That is, these aspirants fail to make enough money to live as they need to, whether at a level of poverty or near-poverty (e.g., the starving artist), passable living or comfortable living (Stebbins 2004/2014, 92–93).

Furthermore, neither type of serious pursuit offers an unalloyed life of positiveness. Both are hugely attractive, even while the enthusiasts invariably face some costs and unpleasant requirements that weigh against the powerful rewards. So it is that, unlike casual leisure, perseverance and effort number among the defining qualities of the serious pursuits.

In the following chapters, I present sets of cases that show how the proposition set out in Stebbins (2004, 73) gives birth to occupational devotion, an interest nurtured in serious leisure. Some participants are so enamored of the core activities of their pursuit that they want to make it their life work (despite the aforementioned disagreeableness). They reach this goal in myriad ways, sometimes as a part-time livelihood and sometimes full-time. Participants may start out as part-time devotee workers and later become full-timers. In this they follow a leisure-work career of growing excellence, fulfillment and, for some, notable respect in the social world in which their activity is embedded. And, alas, occupational devotion, as in the pursuit of serious leisure, can eventuate in career decline, seen in deterioration of skills, creativity, drive to succeed and the like.

There are a variety of personal and social rewards that accrue from engaging in the serious pursuits, which will be set out in Chapter 1. In general, these rewards contribute to the person's self-fulfillment and well-being (Stebbins 2020, 68–69). To find these two super rewards in leisure is perhaps to be expected in certain free-time activities, but at work? Yes, at work. The cases presented in this book attest this fact. They appear in Chapters 2 through 5, each anchored in one of the four sectors of the economy mentioned earlier.

This book is an intellectual journey on leisure as it manifests itself at work. Thus, some favorite concerns in sociology of work such as the definition of professional and craft worker are largely ignored here, likewise with the definition of the various occupations covered in the subsequent chapters. For the definitions of those occupations, I draw instead on the governmental agencies concerned with labor and employment opportunities, the occupations themselves or their commonsense conceptions. These "extra-scholarly" definitions are, by the way, the ones that guide would-be occupational devotees in their quest for fulfilling work. The essential features of the multitude of devotee occupations are set out in Chapter 1 and then applied to each profession, consultancy, trade and small business. The consultancies considered in Chapter 3 were selected for their diversity to show how varied consulting is as an occupation.

Finally, this book is mainly about the importance of leisure in work and much less about work in the wider world. Modern sociology as a discipline gives leisure short shrift, leaving the sociologically inclined scholars in the inter-discipline of leisure studies to make that link (Stebbins 2019). That this book accomplishes this is significant news. From its standpoint, to wander off into a discussion of the place of work in the wider world is to venture beyond its purview.

ACKNOWLEDGMENTS

I am grateful to the staff at Anthem for their careful attention to the myriad editorial details that must be grappled with bringing an academic monograph to life. That attention was also efficiently given, keeping us thereby on the inflexible editing–printing schedule that is the hallmark of this industry. A senior acquisition editor at Anthem worked with similar efficiency to expedite the review and contractual aspects of her role.

Chapter 1

SERIOUS PURSUITS

The present chapter contains the theoretic foundation of this book. Here, I set out the Serious Leisure Perspective (SLP) in detail sufficient to explain occupational devotion. The spotlight will be primarily on amateurs and hobbyists. Consequently, comparatively little will be said about casual leisure and project-based leisure. Volunteering will be considered to the extent that it is a precursor to certain liberal and consulting professions.

The Serious Leisure Perspective

The SLP is the theoretic framework that synthesizes three main forms of leisure, which is accomplished by showing their distinctive features, similarities and interrelationships. Those forms have been labeled *serious leisure* (recently renamed as *serious pursuits* to include *devotee work*), *casual leisure* and *project-based leisure*. They are also shaped by a variety of psychological, social, cultural and historical conditions.

Many of the roots of the Perspective date to late 1973, even though the concept itself was only formally introduced and elaborated much later in Stebbins (2007/2015). It takes its name from serious leisure, mainly because that form was the first to be studied. Research began in 1973 on the first of these (it examined amateurs in classical music and was reported in, among other publications, Stebbins [1976]). Work continued from thereon, consisting of more studies of other amateurs, then various hobbyists, career volunteers, casual leisure participants and enthusiasts attracted to project-based leisure. Within each form, numerous types and subtypes have also emerged over the years. The SLP and the research backing it are discussed in greater detail in Stebbins (2012, 2020).[1]

Additionally, the Perspective considers how the three forms serve as conceptual umbrellas for a range of types of related activities. My research findings and theoretic musings over nearly 50 years have nevertheless evolved, coalescing into a typological map of the domain of leisure. That is, as far as is known at present, all leisure (at least in Western society) can be classified according to one of the three forms and their several types and subtypes. Figure 1.1 portrays the typological structure of the SLP. Note that this is a map, since the reader must go to Stebbins (2012, 2020) to learn what terms like hobbyist, casual leisure and career volunteer mean. In other words, this typology is a *theoretic* rather than a *descriptive* construction. The same holds for Table 1.1, which sets out a typology of volunteers anchored in the SLP. The aspects of the theory behind both constructions that bear on the social world are set out in the remainder of this chapter.

The serious pursuits

We start with the serious leisure component of these pursuits. *Amateurs* are found in art, science, sport and entertainment, where they are invariably linked in a variety of ways with professional counterparts. The two can be distinguished descriptively in that the activity in question constitutes a liveli-hood for professionals but not for amateurs. Furthermore, most professionals work full-time at the activity, whereas most amateurs pursue it part-time. Nonetheless, the two are locked in and therefore further defined, in most instances, by their place in a professional-amateur-public (P-A-P) system of relations, an arrangement too complex to describe further in this book (for details see Stebbins 1979; 1992, 38–41; 2002, 129–30).

Yoder's study (1997) of tournament bass fishing in the United States spawned an important modification of the original P-A-P model. He found, first, that fishers here are amateurs, not hobbyists, and, second, that com-modity producers serving both amateur and professional tournament fishers play a role significant enough to warrant changing the original triangular P-A-P system of relationships first set out in Stebbins (1979). In other words, in the social world of these amateurs, such "strangers" are a highly important group consisting, in the main, of national fishing organizations, tournament promoters and manufacturers and distributors of sporting goods and services. Significant numbers of amateurs make, sell or advertise commodities for the sport. And the professional fishers are supported by the commodity agents by way of paid entry fees for tournaments, provision of boats and fishing tackle and subsidies for living expenses. Top professionals are given a salary to pro-mote fishing commodities. Yoder's (1997, 416) modification results in a more complicated triangular model, consisting of a system of relationships linking commodity agents, professionals/commodity agents and amateurs/publics (C-PC-AP).

The new C-PC-AP model sharpens our understanding of some other ama-teur fields as well. Wilson (1995), for instance, describes a similar, "symbi-otic" relationship between British marathon runners and the media. But, for

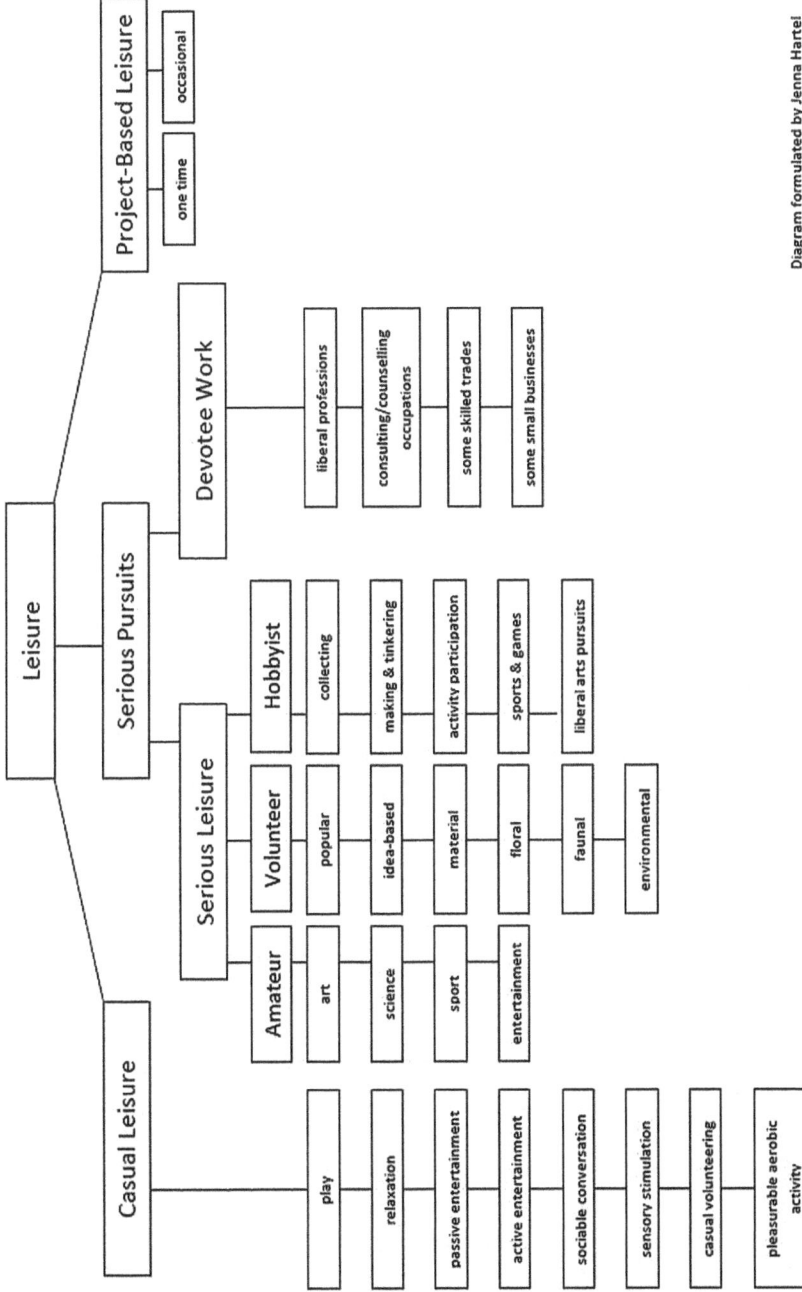

Figure 1.1 The Serious Leisure Perspective

Diagram formulated by Jenna Hartel

Table 1.1 A Leisure-Based Theoretic Typology of Volunteers and Volunteering

	Type of Volunteer		
Leisure Interest	Serious Leisure (SL)	Casual Leisure (CL)	Project-Based Leisure (PBL)
Popular	SL Popular	CL Popular	PBL Popular
Idea-Based	SL Idea-Based	CL Idea-Based	PBL Idea-Based
Material	SL Material	CL Material	PBL Material
Floral	SL Floral	CL Floral	PBL Floral
Faunal	SL Faunal	CL Faunal	PBL Faunal
Environmental	SL Environmental	CL Environmental	PBL Environmental

amateurs in other fields of art, science, sport and entertainment, who are also linked to sets of strangers operating in their special social worlds, we shall see in the next chapter that these strangers play a much more subdued role compared with the four examples just mentioned. Thus, for many amateur activities, the simpler P-A-P model still seems to offer the most valid explanation of their social structure.

But note here that enactment of the core activity by the professionals in a particular field, to influence amateurs there, must be sufficiently visible to those amateurs. If the amateurs, in general, have little or no idea of the prowess of their professional counterparts (e.g., the pros are too rare or too obscure), the latter remain irrelevant as role models, and the leisure side of the activity is experienced at a hobbyist level. This is an economic rather than a sociological definition of "professional." As a result of this reasoning, I have redefined "professional" in economic rather than sociological terms (Stebbins 2007/2015, 6–7) that relate better to amateurs and hobbyists—namely, as someone who is dependent on the income from an activity that other people pursue with little or no remuneration as leisure. The income on which the professional is dependent may be this person's only source of money (i.e., full-time professional) or it may be one of two or more sources of money (i.e., part-time professional). Although some of these professionals may be sociological professionals (as described in Stebbins 1992), many economic professionals are in fields where professionalization is in the sociological sense only beginning.

Hobbyists lack this professional alter ego, suggesting that, historically, all amateurs were hobbyists before their fields professionalized. Both types are drawn to their leisure pursuits significantly more by self-interest than by altruism, whereas volunteers engage in activities requiring a more or less equal blend of these two motives. Hobbyists may be classified into five types: collectors, makers and tinkerers, noncompetitive activity participants (e.g., fishing, hiking, orienteering), hobbyist sports and games (e.g., ultimate

Frisbee, croquet, gin rummy), and the liberal arts hobbies.[2] The liberal arts hobbyists are enamored of the systematic acquisition of knowledge for its own sake. Many of them accomplish this by reading voraciously in a field such as art, sport, cuisine, language, culture, history, science, philosophy, politics or literature (Stebbins 1994). But some of them go beyond this activity to expand their knowledge still further through cultural tourism, documentary videos, television programs and use of similar resources.

Volunteering according to the SLP is un-coerced, intentionally productive, altruistic activity engaged in during free time. Engaged in as leisure, it is, thus, activity that people want to do (Stebbins 2015). It is through volunteer work—done in either a formal or an informal setting—that these people provide a service or benefit to one or more individuals (who must be outside that person's family) or the natural environment (see Table 1.1). Usually, volunteers receive no pay, though people serving in volunteer programs may be compensated for out-of-pocket expenses. Meanwhile, in the typical case, volunteers who are altruistically providing a service or benefit to others are themselves also benefiting from various rewards experienced during this process (e.g., pleasant social interaction, self-enriching experiences, sense of contributing to nonprofit group success). In other words, volunteering is motivated by two basic attitudes: altruism and self-interest (Stebbins 1996).

Serious leisure is rarely significantly remunerative. And this even if a potter sells a vase or two, a racquet-ball player gets paid for giving a handful of lessons, an archaeologist receives a fee for a preconstruction survey of a building site or an amateur pitches batting practice for a local professional team. In some hobbyist sports, including snowboarding, skateboarding and cycling, winners in competitions may receive a monetary prize, perhaps money for an endorsement, doing so often enough to make a living of some kind. But as just observed, the activity does not then become a profession, since this group of elite performers is small (many participants eschew competition; Stebbins 2005a, 65) and limited to the number of paying consumers of such entertainment.

Devotee work

The subject of devotee work, or occupational devotion, has been to this point only sporadically covered. This type of activity is so labeled because the devotees feel a powerful devotion, or strong positive attachment, to a form of self-enhancing work. In such work, the sense of achievement is high, and the core activity endowed with such intense appeal that the line between this work and leisure is virtually erased (Stebbins 2004/2014). In effect, this is serious leisure for which workers get paid and which amounts to a significant part or all of their livelihood.

Occupational devotees turn up chiefly, though not exclusively, in four areas of the economy, providing their work there is, at most, only lightly bureaucratized: certain small businesses, the skilled trades, the consulting and counseling occupations and the public- and client-centered professions. Public-centered professions are found in the arts, sports, scientific and entertainment fields, whereas those who are client-centered abound in such fields as law, teaching, accounting and medicine (Stebbins 1992, 22). It follows from all this that the work and its core activity to which participants become devoted generates for them a respectable personal and social identity within their reference groups, since it would be difficult, if not impossible, to be devoted to work that those groups scorned.

The fact of devotee work for some people and its possibility for others signals that work, as one of life's domains, can be highly positive. Granted, most workers are not fortunate enough to find such work. For those who do find it, the work meets six criteria (Stebbins 2004/2014, 9). To generate occupational devotion:

1. The valued core activity must be profound; to perform it, acceptability requires substantial skill, knowledge or experience or a combination of two or three of these.
2. The core must offer significant variety.
3. The core must also offer significant opportunity for creative or innovative work, as a valued expression of individual personality. The adjectives "creative" and "innovative" stress that the undertaking results in something new or different, showing imagination and application of routine skill or knowledge. That is, boredom is likely to develop only after the onset of fatigue experienced from long hours on the job, a point at which significant creativity and innovation are no longer possible.
4. The would-be devotee must have reasonable control over the amount and disposition of time put into the occupation (the value of freedom of action), such that they can prevent it from becoming a burden. Medium and large bureaucracies have tended to subvert this criterion. For, in interest of the survival and development of their organization, managers have felt they must deny their nonunionized employees this benefit, sometimes forcing them to accept stiff deadlines and heavy workloads. But no activity, be it leisure or work, is so appealing that it invites unlimited participation during all waking hours.
5. The would-be devotee must have both an aptitude and a taste for the work in question. This is, in part, a case of one man's meat being another's poison. John finds great fulfillment in being a physician, an occupation that holds little appeal for Jane who, instead, adores being a lawyer (work John finds unappealing).

6. The devotee must work in a physical and social milieu that encourages them to pursue often and without significant constraint the core activity. This includes freedom from excessive paperwork, caseloads, class sizes, market demands and the like.

Sounds ideal, if not idealistic, but in fact occupations and work roles exist that meet these criteria. In today's climate of occupational deskilling, over-bureaucratization and similar impediments to fulfilling core activity at work, many people find it difficult to locate or arrange devotee employment.

Six qualities

The six qualities listed later characterize both serious leisure and devotee work, giving further substance to the claim put forward here that such leisure and devotee work occupy a great deal of common ground. Together, they comprise the class of serious pursuits. These activities are further defined by six distinctive qualities (sometimes referred to as characteristics), qualities uniformly found among amateurs, hobbyists and volunteers. Sometimes, this is a matter of degree. More precisely, the richest manifestation of the six is found in these pursuits, with weak or diluted manifestation or none at all being evident in the casual and project-based activities. For example, even in the serious pursuits, neophytes are unlikely to put in the levels of effort and perseverance that moderate devotees do.

Thus, there is the occasional need to *persevere*. Participants who want to continue experiencing the same level of fulfillment in the activity have to meet certain challenges from time to time. Another quality sharply distinguishing all the serious pursuits is the opportunity to follow a (leisure, or leisure-devotee work) *career* in the endeavor, a career shaped by its own special contingencies, turning points and stages of achievement and involvement (the most extensive treatment now found in Stebbins 2014). Moreover, most, if not all, careers here owe their existence to a third quality: Serious leisure participants make significant personal *effort* using their specially acquired knowledge, training or skill and, indeed at times, all three. Careers for serious leisure participants unfold along lines of their efforts to achieve, for instance, a high level of showmanship, athletic prowess or scientific knowledge or to accumulate formative experiences in a volunteer role.

The serious pursuits are further distinguished by several *durable benefits* or tangible, salutary outcomes such activity has for its participants. They include self-actualization, self-enrichment, self-expression, self-fulfillment, regeneration or renewal of self, feelings of accomplishment, enhancement of self-image, social interaction and sense of belonging and lasting physical products of the activity (e.g., a painting, scientific paper, piece of furniture). A further benefit—self-gratification, or pure fun, which is by far the most evanescent benefit in this list—is also enjoyed by casual leisure participants. The possibility of realizing such benefits constitutes a powerful goal in the serious pursuits.

Fifth, each serious pursuit is distinguished by a unique and complex *ethos and social world* that emerges in parallel with each expression of it. An ethos is the spirit of the community of serious leisure/devotee work participants, as manifested in shared context of attitudes, practices, values, beliefs, goals and so on. The social world of the participants is the organizational milieu in which the associated ethos—at bottom, a cultural formation—is expressed (as attitudes, beliefs, values) or realized (as practices, goals). The complexity of this ethos is also a matter of degree, meaning that empirical and theoretical cutoff points separating casual leisure and serious pursuits must be established statistically using, for example, the Serious Leisure Inventory and Measure developed by Gould et al. (2008) or the 21-item scale of Tsaur and Liang (2008).

According to David Unruh (1979, 1980), every social world has its characteristic groups, events, routines, practices and organizations. It is held together, to an important degree, by semiformal, or mediated, communication. In other words, in the typical case, social worlds are neither heavily bureaucratized nor substantially organized through intense face-to-face interaction. Rather, communication is commonly mediated by newsletters, posted notices, telephone messages, mass mailings, radio and television announcements and similar means.

Every social world contains four types of members: strangers, tourists, regulars and insiders (Unruh 1979, 1980). The strangers are intermediaries who normally participate little in the leisure/work activity itself but who nonetheless do something important to make it possible, for example, by managing municipal parks (in amateur baseball), minting coins (in hobbyist coin collecting) and organizing the work of teachers' aides (in career volunteering). Tourists are temporary participants in a social world; they have come on the scene momentarily for entertainment, diversion or profit. Most amateur and hobbyist activities have publics of some kind, which are, at bottom, constituted of tourists. The clients of many volunteers can be similarly classified. The regulars routinely participate in the social world; in the serious pursuits, they are the amateurs, hobbyists, volunteers and devotee workers themselves. The insiders are those among them who show exceptional devotion to the social world they share, to maintaining it, to advancing it (see involvement scale in Stebbins 2014, 32–33, or at www.seriousleisure.net). Scott and McMahan (2017) describe in detail these exceptional participants who engage in "hardcore" leisure.

Unruh's four types of members attest the complexity of this formation and what, therefore, must be done to portray decently the social world of any given leisure activity. In other words, these four types are interrelated in diverse and often subtle ways, demanding thus close ethnographic examination of them. Complex social worlds spring up around complex leisure activities, namely, those animating the serious pursuits. The complexity of the latter is evident in the diversity of their groups and organizations, events, facilities for pursuing the core activities, resources and so forth.

The sixth quality—participants in serious leisure tend to identify strongly with their chosen pursuits—springs from the presence of the other five distinctive qualities. In contrast, most casual leisure, although not usually humiliating or despicable, is nonetheless too fleeting, mundane and commonplace to become the basis for a distinctive *identity* for most people. Some of the benefits (e.g., sense of belonging, self-gratification), aspects of a social world and identity are also found in casual leisure, albeit in comparatively watered-down form. In other words, notable perseverance and effort linked to a sharp sense of leisure career and durable benefits all of which are framed in the social world and ethos of the activity underlie the distinctive identity that emerges.

Rewards and costs

The main way that the serious pursuits are set off from other kinds of work and leisure is by the extraordinary rewards they offer. These rewards act as powerful motives for being involved in one or more of those pursuits. Still, the serious pursuits are also distinguished by the fact that participants sometimes encounter costs while engaging in them. It is this profile of rewards and costs that places the serious pursuits at odds with the popular images of work as drudgery and leisure as an unalloyed good time. To repeat, this is why my interviewees kept underscoring that their leisure was out of the ordinary, not like that of most other people, they said.

The rewards of a serious leisure pursuit are the more or less routine values that attract and hold its enthusiasts. Every serious leisure career both frames and is framed by the continuous search for these rewards. Moreover, this search may take months, and in some fields years, before the participant consistently finds self-fulfillment in their amateur, hobbyist or volunteer activity. Ten rewards have so far emerged in the course of the various studies of amateurs, hobbyists and career volunteers. As the following list shows, the rewards are predominantly personal.

Personal rewards
1. Personal enrichment (cherished experiences)
2. Self-actualization (developing skills, abilities, knowledge)
3. Self-expression (expressing skills, abilities, knowledge already developed)

4. Self-image (known to others as a particular kind of serious leisure participant)
5. Self-gratification (combination of superficial enjoyment and deep fulfillment)
6. Re-creation (regeneration) of oneself through serious leisure after a day's work
7. Financial return (from a serious leisure activity)

Social rewards
8. Social attraction (associating with other serious leisure participants, with clients as a volunteer, participating in the social world of the activity)
9. Group accomplishment (group effort in accomplishing a serious leisure project; senses of helping, being needed, being altruistic)
10. Contribution to the maintenance and development of the group (including senses of helping, being needed, being altruistic in making the contribution)

In the various studies on amateurs, hobbyists and volunteers, these rewards, depending on the activity, were often given different weightings by research interviewees to reflect their importance relative to each other. Nonetheless, some common ground exists, for the studies do show that, in terms of their personal importance, most serious leisure participants rank self-enrichment as number one and self-gratification as number two. Moreover, to find either reward, participants must have acquired sufficient levels of relevant skill, knowledge and experience and be in a position to use these acquisitions (Stebbins 1979, 1993a). In other words, self-actualization, which was often ranked third in importance, is also highly rewarding in serious leisure.

It is in order to interject at this point a brief aside on terminology. As mentioned earlier, I have in recent years taken to using the concept of *fulfillment* (Stebbins 2004a). It points to a fulfilling experience, or more precisely, to a set of chronological experiences leading to development to the fullest of a person's gifts and character, to development of that person's full potential. Such an acquisition is certainly both a reward and a benefit of serious leisure. Rewards 1 through 3 are manifestations of fulfillment.

Satisfaction, the term I once used, sometimes refers to a satisfying experience that is fun or enjoyable (also referred to as gratifying). In another sense, this noun may refer to meeting or satisfying a need or want. In neither instance does satisfaction denote the preferred sense of fulfillment just presented. In general, satisfaction is commonly what we gain from casual leisure, whereas fulfillment typically comes with its serious counterpart. Reward 5 sometimes brings the enthusiast both, as in the jazz musician who had "fun" at the jam session (i.e., it was fun to play well while developing further as an artist).

Finally, note that both rewards and costs were mentioned by the interviewees during my research into their serious pursuits. More particularly, they saw their leisure as a mix of rewards offsetting costs as experienced in the central activity. Moreover, every serious pursuit contains its own combination of these costs, which each participant must confront in some way. So far, it has been impossible to develop a general list of them, as has been done for the rewards. The reason seems to be that the costs tend to be highly specific to each activity. In general terms, the costs discovered to date may be classified as *disappointments*, *dislikes* or *tensions*. Thus, it can be disappointing to fail to place in a sports contest, to be able to afford a treasured antique for one's collection or to paint a landscape as the artists believe it should be done. Dislikes arise in the serious pursuits when, for instance, an umpire makes what players regard as a bad call, a weekend rain spoils the backpacking trip or a book's price discourages a hobbyist reader from purchasing it. The tensions tend to be interpersonal, as in community orchestra conductors who lambaste the playing of a section, friction between volunteer coordinators and the volunteers whom they direct or disagreements with the management of a recreation center that provides racket ball and badminton courts.

Casual leisure

Casual leisure is immediately intrinsically rewarding, relatively short-lived pleasurable activity requiring little or no special training to enjoy it. It is fundamentally hedonic, pursued for its significant level of pure enjoyment or pleasure. I coined the term in the first conceptual statement about serious leisure (Stebbins 1982a), which at the time depicted its casual counterpart as all activity not classifiable as serious (nor as project-based leisure, which I subsequently identified as a third form; see the next section). Casual leisure is considerably less substantial than serious leisure, while offering no career of the sort found in the latter. Its types—there are eight (see Figure 1.1)—include play (e.g., dabbling, doodling, daydreaming), relaxation (e.g., sitting, napping, strolling), passive entertainment (e.g., popular TV, videos, books, recorded music), active entertainment (e.g., games of chance, party games), sociable conversation (e.g., gossiping, joking, talking about the weather), sensory stimulation (e.g., sex, eating, drinking, sightseeing) and casual volunteering (as opposed to career, volunteering). Casual volunteering includes handing out leaflets, stuffing envelopes and collecting money door-to-door. Note that dabbling (as play) may occur in the same genre of activity pursued by amateurs, hobbyists and career volunteers. The last and newest type of casual leisure—pleasurable aerobic activity—refers to physical activities that require effort sufficient to cause marked increase in respiration and heart rate. As applied here, the term "aerobic activity" is broad in scope, encompassing all activity that calls for such effort, which includes exercise routines pursued collectively in (narrowly conceived of) aerobics classes and those pursued individually by way of televised or recorded programs of aerobics (Stebbins 2004b). Yet, as with its passive and active cousins in entertainment, pleasurable aerobic activity is basically casual leisure. That is, to do such activity requires little more than minimal skill, knowledge or experience. Examples include the game of the Hash House Harriers (a type of treasure hunt in the outdoors), kickball, "exergames" for children (videogames that center on physical activity like dancing) and children's pastimes such as hide-and-seek.

Project-based leisure

Although systematic exploration may reveal others, two types of project-based leisure have so far been identified: one-off projects and occasional projects (Stebbins 2005b).

One-off projects

In all these projects, people generally use the talents and knowledge they have at hand, even though for some projects they may seek certain instructions beforehand, including reading a book or manual or taking a short, adult-education style course. And some projects resembling hobbyist activity participation may require a modicum of preliminary conditioning. Always, the goal is to undertake successfully the one-off project and nothing more, and sometimes a small amount of background preparation is necessary for this. It is possible that a survey would show that most project-based leisure is hobbyist in character, the next most common is a kind of volunteering. The third most common are the arts projects.

Occasional projects

The occasional projects seem more likely to originate in or be motivated by agreeable obligation than their one-off cousins. Examples of occasional projects include the sum of the culinary, decorative or other creative activities undertaken, for example, at home or at work for a religious occasion or someone's birthday. Likewise, national holidays and similar celebratory occasions sometimes inspire individuals to mount occasional projects consisting of an ensemble of inventive elements.

Conclusions

In the foregoing pages, the distinctive quality of career stands out as a bridge concept between leisure and work, starting as it does is serious leisure (sometimes even casual leisure) and continuing in devotee work. Career will find its way into each of the following chapters. But further conceptualizing of this central idea will occur at the beginning of the next chapter.

Notes

1   For a brief history of the Perspective, see the history page at www.seriousleisure.net or, for a longer version, see Stebbins (2007/2015, chap. 6).
2   These activities are inherently noncompetitive, even while individuals might compete as to who reaches the mountain top first, catches the most fish or the biggest one, seen the greatest variety of birds and so on.

Chapter 2

LIBERAL PROFESSIONS

The liberal professions begin in cognate amateur and volunteer pursuits. Discussion in this chapter is organized according to the public-centered professions (in art, science, sport, entertainment) and their client-centered counterparts (e.g., law, medicine, education, architecture, engineering). Amateurism in the latter type is pursued in the educational programs leading to professional certification, given that, to practice in these fields, its practitioners must acquire such validation.

The liberal professions discussed later constitute a sample of the total of such occupations in modern Western society. The principal object is to present an *apercu* of each that both describes it and its activities and shows how it conforms to the six criteria for occupational devotion. The sample is meant to be representative of the liberal professions, though limited to those on which there is some qualitative research or online information on their nature.

Public-Centered Professions

Pursuit of these professions tends to conform to the involvement scale that was introduced 30 years ago (Stebbins 1992, 46–48). There I observed that, at any point in time, serious leisure enthusiasts may be classified as either *devotees* or *participants*. The devotees (later some may become occupational devotees) are highly dedicated to their pursuits, whereas the participants are only moderately interested in it, albeit significantly more so than casual leisure dabblers. Participants typically greatly outnumber devotees. Along this dimension, devotees and participants are operationally differentiated primarily by the different amounts of time they commit to their serious leisure, as manifested in engaging in the core activity, training or preparing for it, reading about it and similar indicators.

This was, however, a rather crude scale of intensity of involvement in a serious leisure activity, a weakness not missed by Siegenthaler and O'Dell (2003). Their findings from a study of older golfers and successful aging revealed that data on leisure career are more effectively considered according to three types, labeled by them as "social," "moderate" and "core devotee." The moderate is equivalent to the participant, whereas the social player falls into a class of players who are more skilled and involved than dabblers but less skilled and involved than the moderates (participants). To keep terminology consistent with past theory and research and the generality of the earlier two terms, I have suggested that we calibrate this new, more detailed, involvement scale with appropriate new terms: *participant, moderate devotee* and *core devotee* (Stebbins 2007/2015, 21). Moreover, the scale should include neophytes and, as precursors, dabblers and participants in project-based leisure. This expanded Serious Leisure Perspective (SLP) Involvement Scale is presented in Figure 2.1. Considering this involvement scale and the CL-SL continuum together has a number of advantages. For instance, they bring casual leisure and dabbling to the fore by also focusing attention on the process of either deciding to become or drifting toward becoming a neophyte in a serious leisure activity. More particularly, the continuum now gives full recognition to casual and project-based leisure as *possible* preliminary steps in the process of choosing and pursuing a leisure activity.

We must remember, however, that movement along the CL-SL continuum is by no means inevitable. Thus, many a casual leisure activity holds little or no possibility of leading on to a career in serious leisure. Included in this list are relaxation (e.g., napping, strolling in the park), sensory stimulation

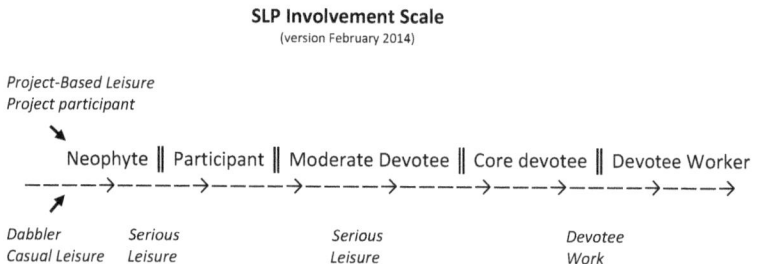

SLP Involvement Scale
(version February 2014)

Project-Based Leisure
Project participant

Neophyte ‖ Participant ‖ Moderate Devotee ‖ Core devotee ‖ Devotee Worker

Dabbler   *Serious*   *Serious*   *Devotee*
Casual Leisure   *Leisure*   *Leisure*   *Work*

Notes:
- Level of involvement may peak at any point on this scale.
- Some dabblers and project participants never become neophytes.
- Some neophytes before their involvement neither dabbled nor participated in a project.

Figure 2.1 Serious Leisure Perspective Involvement Scale

Notes:
- Level of involvement may peak at any point on this scale.
- Some dabblers and project participants never become neophytes.
- Some neophytes before their involvement neither dabbled nor participated in a project. (version February 2014)

(e.g., sex, sightseeing, drinking alcohol) and casual volunteering (e.g., handing out leaflets on a street corner, taking tickets for a performance of an amateur play). Furthermore, even with their casual interest in an activity capable of being pursued seriously, some participants never become neophytes. How many people, children included, simply forever dabble at tennis, bird watching, swimming or playing the piano? Meanwhile, activities exist that are so complex, require so much initial skill and knowledge, that entering them, even to participate minimally, is only possible with significant training and knowledge. Quilters, ski jumpers, sky divers, oboe players and ballet dancers, for example, have to acquire a rudimentary level of competence before they can begin to do their activity, even at its simplest. They enter the CL-SL continuum as neophytes, bypassing altogether the exploratory delights of casual leisure dabbling.

In the careers of the occupational devotees discussed in this chapter, the career line most often begins at the amateur level in an art, sport, science or entertainment.

Arts

We turn first to music. Musicians and singers, both amateur and professional, play instruments or sing, many doing so before live audiences with some performing in recording studios. These artists often work in such settings as concert halls, arenas and nightclubs, but rehearse in a diversity of more exclusive locations, including someone's home or garage or rental space available at a church, school or municipal arts center (on rehearsals, see Juniu et al. 1996). They may also give recitals, educational presentations and perform at a variety of social gatherings, for example, receptions, weddings and tourist attractions. Some work for tips as buskers on street corners, subway thoroughfares, community parks and the like.

Musicians and singers interested in performing popular music typically do so without postsecondary education and training. It is different for many performers of classical music and opera who must have at least a bachelor's degree. These artists need extensive training and regular practice to acquire the theory, skills, knowledge and experience necessary to interpret music at a professional or advanced amateur level. Vocalists may sing a cappella or with musical accompaniment. Trained musicians often interpret or modify music and apply their knowledge of harmony, melody, rhythm and voice production to individualize presentations and stimulate audience interest. Further, some in this category specialize in playing a family of instruments (e.g., percussion, reeds, keyboards) or a type of music (e.g., baroque, small group jazz, folk, country-western).

A major question, still without answer throughout the arts, is how many serious or moderately serious amateurs begin to consider their art as a possible part-time or full-time livelihood? Further, when in life does this question arise: late adolescence, mid-life, early old age? In general, we lack the data with which to provide answers, except to note that most musicians, painters, dancers, actors and so on have as their goal a full-time living at the end of their postsecondary education and training (on music, see Henderson and Spracklen 2014; Ramirez 2019). Kuusi and Haukola (2017) also have some preliminary findings bearing on these questions.

Artistic painting and sculpting

Turning first to the artists, who commonly paint on paper, canvas, glass, objects, wood panels and still other surfaces or who work with silk screen or prefer watercolor or charcoal over pigment or ink. The works are classified as portraits, landscapes, abstractions, still life, emotive, activist (political), among several other genres. Most artists use small brushes, whereas some also work with knives, sponges or airbrushes (including aerosols for graffiti).[1] Sculptors learn how to create designs for their three-dimensional creations and determine the necessary materials and techniques to accomplish this. The term as used here refers to large works (e.g., statues, something attached to a building, free-standing abstractions) and to hand- and table-top sized pieces.

As amateurs, these artists learn how to create drawings, paintings and other original works. Critical here is how to visualize and capture the relationships of all elements that form an artistic whole, including how to represent three-dimensional objects on two-dimensional surfaces. This includes learning how to harmonize relationships of line, color, design and mass into unified aesthetic arrangements. In both painting and sculpting, one must develop motor coordination and finger dexterity when using small paint brushes and diverse sculpting tools (used for cutting, scraping, shaping, smoothing and detailing such material as clay, wood, ice and stone).

Creative ability and talent are the trademark of these arts, as demonstrated by a portfolio of original work and knowledge of the safe use of materials, tools and equipment. These qualities are often evident at the preprofessional amateur level serving to motivate these participants to seek a career in painting or sculpting. Art programs are offered at many universities, colleges and private art schools, successful completion of which is increasingly the sine qua non of professional status. Amateurs aspiring to make a living in art or sculpting view these programs as a main stepping stone in their occupational career, typically one of self-employment. See Brett-MacLean (2007) on artists starting their careers late in life and Marnin-Distelfeld (2020) on the transition from amateur to professional in art. A similar devotee leisure-to-work pattern has been observed in photography (Yang 2021).

Dance and choreography

Dancers and choreographers use dance performances to express ideas and stories. Dance is a performing art consisting of selected sequences of human movement. This movement has aesthetic and symbolic value and is recognized as dance by the performers and their audiences as it is framed in a particular culture. Dance can be categorized and described by its choreography, by its repertoire of movements or by its historical period or place of origin (see also McQuarrie and Jackson 1996).

Covered here are the forms of concert or theater dance, done while omitting social dance exemplified as square dancing, line dancing and morris dancing. The social dances show little professionalization, whereas concert dancing like ballet, jazz, tap, modern and ballroom dance have pure amateur and then preprofessional amateur career stages that push some enthusiasts toward devotee work (Schupp 2020; Stevens-Ratchford 2016).[2]

Some dancers work in performing arts companies, whereas others are self-employed. It is likewise with choreographers who may also work in dance schools or freelance as self-employed artists. Education and training requirements vary with the type of dancer. Although all dancers need many years of formal training, they first develop their passion for the art as pure amateurs and continue to do so as preprofessionals. Moreover, nearly all choreographers begin their careers as dancers, doing so through their formal training or beyond as professionals. Dance studies are offered in a variety of arts and humanities programs at many postsecondary institutions, with some of them also offering postgraduate degrees in this field.

Writing

This section centers on the artist identified as a writer defined as follows:

> A *writer* is a person who uses written words in different styles and techniques to communicate ideas. Writers produce different forms of literary art and creative writing such as novels, short stories, books, poetry, plays, screenplays, teleplays, songs, and essays as well as other reports and news articles that may be of interest to the public. Writers' texts are published across a range of media. ("Writer," *Wikipedia*, retrieved March 20, 2021).

A college or university degree in English (or the language the writer works in), communications or journalism is generally required for a full-time position as a writer or author. Experience gained through internships or any writing that improves skill, such as blogging, is helpful. This said, many writers appear to start as amateurs in high school, contributing copy to the school newspaper, blogging, writing commentaries about experiences, course-based essays and the like. At this stage, they learn to choose subjects of interest to readers, a basic ingredient for success in this art.

Adult amateurs and professionals write fiction or nonfiction scripts, poetry, biographies, essays and other formats. In formal essays, authors present their own arguments on a range of subjects, projects that may require research to gather factual information in authentic detail. Some professionals write advertising copy for newspapers, magazines, broadcasts and the internet or work with editors and clients to shape material for publishing. Still, for the writers of *belles lettres*, professional careers can be elusive (see Stiénon 2008 and, on poets, see Craig 2007).

Acting

Acting takes place in a theater or other stage-like setting as a collaborative form of a performing art. It uses live performers, usually actors (actresses included), to present the experience of a real or imagined event before a live audience in a specific place, often a stage. The performers may communicate this experience to the audience through combinations of gesture, speech, song, music and dance.

Many professional actors get their appetite for theater whetted through dramatic activities in high school (e.g., speeches, class plays, special skits). The principal types of theater are plays, musical theater, public speaking, stand-up comedy, opera, mime and entertainment magic. The latter four are not usually available in high schools but must be sought in the local community (comedy, magic) or in selected post-secondary institutions (opera, mime) often located elsewhere in the country.

What does the activity of acting consist of? Actors, amateurs and professional, express ideas and portray characters in theater, film, television and other performing arts media. They interpret a writer's script to entertain or inform an audience. They do this in various settings, including theaters (for amateurs and pros) and mainly for the latter, production studios, theaters and theme parks, or on location. As work or leisure, assignments are usually short, ranging from a day to a few months

Many actors enhance their skills through formal dramatic education (often leading to a bachelor's degree), and long-term training is common. They read scripts and meet with agents and other professionals before accepting a role. Typically, they audition in front of directors, producers and casting directors.

Additionally, they must study and research their character's personal traits and circumstances to authentically portray the characters to an audience. Lines, of course, must be memorized and performed in rehearsals with other actors, whether on stage or in front of a camera. During this rehearsal period, the actors discuss their role with the director, producer and other actors to improve the overall performance of the show. They then present their roles onstage according to the director's directions.

Science

Amateurs are found in significant numbers in the following sciences: astronomy, archaeology, history, entomology, ornithology, mineralogy, botany and meteorology. These citizen scientists, who are predominantly observers bent on exploration and description, vary much more than their professional counterparts in their level of knowledge and degree of ability and willingness to contribute original data to their science. Thus, these observers pursue their scientific activity as one of three subtypes whom I have dubbed apprentices, journeypeople and masters (Stebbins 1980). Moreover, some of them find that their leisure career in their science has them advancing from apprentice to journeyperson and possibly on to master.[3] Such passage is an inexact process, however, for the acquisition of knowledge, experience and personal confidence is always gradual and at times hesitant.

Scientific apprentices are learners. They hope to absorb enough about their discipline, its research procedures and its instrumentation to function as a journeyperson and eventually, possibility, as a master. As their knowledge about the science grows, some apprentices select a specialty, becoming learners here as well. Scientific apprentices, unlike their opposite number in the trades, are normally independent; for example, formal association with a master over a prescribed period of time is unheard of. Even at this stage, these practitioners have the freedom to explore their science on their own, which they do mostly by reading and listening to talks. At this point, however, they are typically incapable of making an original contribution to it.

journeypeople are knowledgeable, reliable practitioners who can work independently in one or a few specialties. They have advanced far enough to make original contributions to their science. Yet, it is a matter of personal definition as to whether an amateur has reached this level of expertise. The amateurs I interviewed were typically modest, even humble, about their attainments. They seemed to sense when they were effectively apprentices, when they had much to learn and when they needed supervision in, say, excavating an archaeological site or needed more experience in working up a valid set of observations. Even journeypeople may feel "inadequate" after comparing themselves with the local professionals with whom a number of them have frequent contact. journeypeople are always learning, expanding their grasp of the discipline as a whole and absorbing new developments pertaining to their specialty. The same holds for the masters as well as the professionals.

The masters actually contribute to their science, most often by collecting original data on their own that help advance the field. They are aware of certain knowledge gaps in their specialties, and they know how to make the observations that could conceivably close or at least narrow those gaps. To this end, they systematically collect the relevant data and publicize them through talks, reports and journal articles. Any amateur can contribute through serendipity such as by fortuitously discovering a new celestial object. But masters systematically seek new data through programs they design (e.g., digging their own archaeological sites) or coordinate with others (e.g., working as part of a team positioned geographically to observe a lunar occultation).

Master amateur research projects are chiefly exploratory and descriptive, however, with the theorizing and hypotheses-testing being left to the pros. Nevertheless, when these projects are properly carried out, validation of the researcher's status as a master follows. Amateurs and professionals alike acknowledge the individual's contributions, journal articles are accepted for publication and the occasional local speaking invitation may be received. In these fields, the professionals recognize the existence of amateurs, and some of them welcome their scientific contributions. Their love for this level of descriptive/exploratory research tends to discourage amateurs from seeking a professional outlet for their passion, which in any case, would usually require a PhD.

Amateur contributions in astronomy result from such activities as describing variable stars, occultations of stars, double stars, sunspots and occasional discoveries of comets and astronomical events, for example. Contributions made by amateur archaeologists who usually pursue their science locally center on the physical remains of past peoples in history and their activities as are available through excavation (Stebbins 1979; Taylor 1995). Amateur historians are mostly specialists in an earlier aspect of a particular community or somewhat larger region (e.g., prominent families or individuals, important events, social or environmental trends). See Piskunova (2010) on Russian amateur historians. Amateur entomology often revolves around monitoring and getting to know local species of insects, putting the participant in an excellent position to spot unusual population changes that may reflect environmental trends. In ornithology, masters-level amateurs contribute in a multitude of ways, such as by helping with annual bird counts, installing leg and wing bands and observing territoriality and nest-fidelity.

The website Bluespan (2016) explains how some amateur meteorologists can make valuable contributions to their science:

If you are interested in amateur meteorology, getting started is easier than you might think. There are a number of highly-rated personal weather stations on the market which can send your unit's collected information directly to observer websites.

The premade personal weather stations use a number of sensors to read different types of information. These sensors include thermocouples, thermistors, hygrometers, barometers, rain gauges, and anemometers, all of which work together to provide details about current and upcoming weather.

Amateur observers measure wind, temperature, and rain, recording those numbers, study weather patterns, and make predictions based on that information. When you have compiled your stats, it can then be uploaded to websites and added to weather maps and forecasts.

The advent of the internet has greatly enhanced amateurism in this science, which features an in-depth understanding of local weather (see Morris and Endfield 2012). Concerning amateur mycologists, they are not only gatherers of mushrooms (for eating) but also masters who collect data of use to the science of mycology. Gary Fine (1998, 223) found that professional mycologists sometimes ask committed amateurs to provide specimens of a certain mushroom available in the region where the latter live. In general, the amateurs' interests revolve around the taxonomy and morphology of fleshy fungi, discovered anomalies of which stir professional interest.

The evidence to date suggests that the amateurs in astronomy (Stebbins 1982b), archaeology (Stebbins 1979) and mycology (Fine 1998; Watling 1998) have little interest in becoming occupational devotees, including getting the advanced education needed to do this (i.e., graduate study). But on astronomers, see Orchiston (2014). I could find no information on this question for amateur meteorologists, who conceivably might find professional work to their amateur liking. In fact, many free-time involvements in some of the scientific fields are not amateur at all but rather of the hobbyist collector variety (of rocks, insects, fungi, etc.).

Sport

The Shorter Oxford English Dictionary, 5th edition (2002), defines sport as "an activity involving physical exertion and skill in which an individual or a team competes against another or others to achieve the best performance." For the SLP, and hence this book, the critical point in this definition is that sport always involves competition with one or more other people. Challenges posed by nature—the "nature challenge activities" (Davidson and Stebbins 2011)—fall outside this definition of sport, since human competitors are not involved. When they are involved as sometimes happens in skiing, cycling over a course and racing in sail boats, the activity is properly analyzed as a sport.

It follows that the nature challenge activities, most of which are classified in the SLP as hobbies, are not covered here. As such there are few if any professionals whom one might emulate, though winners in some nature challenge contests do take home a purse. But even here the amount of money and frequency of its availability fall short of constituting a livelihood, of sustaining the winner at any professional level.

Team sport

The team sports offering a career leading to occupational devotion are the following: football/soccer, rugby, baseball, basketball and ice hockey. Descriptions of these sports are available in all the larger encyclopedias and online sites dedicated to the various sports. Careers in sport typically start during childhood or adolescence at the latest. Early on, most everyone who tries out for a local team is accepted as a member. As players age, however, competition for a place on the best of them (for that age group) grows more intense, in part, because the number of top-level teams is shrinking. Players aspiring for professional work must strive mightily to gain entry into these groups, which are often age-graded (e.g., 12–13 years, 17–20 years). From such teams, the best of their members often hope to be "drafted" to play on a professional team (exemplified in Canadian football, Stebbins 1993b, and in ice hockey, MacCosham and Gravelle 2017).

Individual sport

Tennis is one of the best known in this category. Like players of other individual sports, such as golf, they are not salaried, but to obtain prize money, they must play in tournaments and place well there. Most large tournaments seed players, but players may also be matched by their skill level. According to how well an individual does in sanctioned play, that person is given a rating (by a tennis organization), which is adjusted periodically to maintain competitive matches. These pros are not paid a salary, as happens in professional team sport, but live off of prizes from tournaments and, secondarily, from endorsements and, if well-known, gifts of clothing and equipment. Muir (1991) and Lim and Lee (2013) describe the passion of the serious tennis players, an important precursor of their movement into the professional ranks.

The majority of professional golfers work as club or teaching professionals ("pros") and compete only in local competitions. A small elite of professional golfers are "tournament pros" who compete full-time on international "tours." Many club and teaching pros working in the golf industry start as caddies or with a general interest in the game then find employment at golf courses. From here, they may move on to certification as coaches or as instructors in their chosen profession. These certification programs are offered by independent organizations and universities and can eventually lead to a Class-A professional certification in golf. Touring professionals typically start as amateur players, who attain pro status after success in major tournaments from which they win prize money or recognition from corporate sponsors, if not both (see "Golf," *Wikipedia*, retrieved March 25, 2021).

Amateur boxing in the UK and the United States took root in the nineteenth and early twentieth centuries. Young men and late adolescent males joined clubs that organized lessons, matches and tournaments. Many a university had boxing teams that competed in intercollegiate matches. There were also military-based clubs and teams. A boxer's rating determines that person's eligibility to participate in world championship fights and is thus linked closely to the amount of money that can be earned. All the professional boxing organizations, such as the World Boxing Council (WBC), the World Boxing Association (WBA) and the International Boxing Federation (IBF), rank boxers. Sales of tickets to matches and then the availability of television programming also greatly increased boxing revenues, particularly events broadcast via closed-circuit television and, later, pay-for-view events on cable. Million-dollar purses for heavyweight championships became commonplace by the 1970s, and the then heavyweight champion Mohamed Ali earned an estimated $69 million during his 20-year professional career. By the 1980s, multimillion-dollar purses were no longer available only to the heavyweight division.

For most fighters, an amateur career, especially at the Olympics, serves to develop skills and gain experience in preparation for a professional career. Western boxers typically participate in one Olympics and then turn pro, Cubans and other socialist countries have an opportunity to collect multiple medals. ("Boxing," *Wikipedia*, retrieved March 26, 2021; see also Ribeiro 2017)

Ten-pin bowling is well-developed in the United States, where the Amateur Bowling Tour organizes nationally annual tournaments with prize money given to the first-place contestant. Meanwhile, the Professional Bowling Association currently operates with ten teams of five players and each playing in an annual tournament in which all individual participants are guaranteed a one-time payment large enough to support a decent living for a year. In fact, of the individual sports covered here, ten-pin bowling in the United States offers one of the clearest paths to professional status from amateurism.

Entertainment

In common sense, one principal meaning of the verb "to entertain" is to provide a public with something enjoyable, or pleasurable, that holds their attention for the period of time the entertaining object or occasion is perceived. In entertainment that truly entertains (recognizing that some would-be entertainment "flops"), attention is diverted from all other matters, hence occasional usage of one of its synonyms: diversion (Stebbins 2007, 178). Entertainers, as studied in the sociology of entertainment, have been either amateur or professional, with both holding a commercial orientation toward their art. That is, the professionals develop a product designed to sell to a public, while the amateurs, though they often perform without pay, model their products on professional exemplars.

All the arts covered earlier in this chapter have commercial wings intended to serve as popular fare, as entertainment. Thus, we have popular music as seen in rock and country western, popular theatre as seen in stand-up comedy and entertainment magic, popular dance as seen in disco and salsa, popular writing as seen in *50 Shades of Grey* and *The Handmaid's Tale* and popular photography as seen in travel and wild life photography. The training to be an entertainer, whether formal or informal, is much the same as that for the arts noncommercial counterpart: learning the basics, the theory and technique of making music, acting, dancing, writing or taking photographs. Still, these are artistic fields of devotee work, even while their publics view them as sources of casual hedonic pleasure.

Agency is paramount in this area, being most evident on its informal side. There is little formal schooling available for the entertainment branch of these arts. Stand-up comics, for instance, commonly get their start observing this art being performed in comedy clubs, eventually writing their own material which they present there during "open mic" nights (Stebbins 1990). Advice from professionals augments this on-the-job training. Nonetheless, some amateurs may learn their art at the American Comedy Institute (New York), San Francisco Comedy College, or the Humber College Comedy Program (Toronto). Successful amateurs eventually get a chance to present the opening act in a weekend show and, from there, start their transition toward professional status by hiring a booking agent and later gaining more central billing at various comedy clubs, fairs, festivals and the like.

Amateur entertainment magicians school themselves by reading manuals and pamphlets on presenting their art to adults or children, watching videos and DVDs about magic tricks, reading histories and biographies on the great performers in the field and by attending (usually local) conferences and workshops, joining magic clubs and so on (Nardi, 1984;Stebbins 1993a). At first, the amateurs make little or no money at their art, often presenting it gratis at children's birthday parties. Later, as adults and sometimes with the help of an agent, they find a living working at events, nightclubs, special parties, variety shows, fairs and festivals, among other opportunities.

Clowning (theatre) and ventriloquism

Members of Clowns of America, Inc. (COAI) get access to educational materials and mentors who can help them learn more about clowning. These neophytes also receive a bimonthly magazine called *The New Calliope* filled with articles, pictures, ideas, as well as advertisements for different dealers, camps and convention opportunities. This organization also offers occasional workshops online by way of Zoom. The goal of the COAI website (https://mycoai.com/) is to share, educate and act as a gathering place for serious amateur, semi-professional and professional clowns. It provides its members with the necessary resources that enable them to further define and improve their individual clown character.

Ventriloquism's popularity waned for a while, evident in the UK in 2010 where there were only 15 full-time professional ventriloquists, down from around 400 in the 1950s and '60s ("Ventriloquism," *Wikipedia*, retrieved March 28, 2021). But popularity of the art has picked up since then. In general, the majority of ventriloquists are self-employed. They are hired by businesses and other organizations to travel and perform. Most are paid an hourly rate for their time. Other ventriloquists, however, work on more formal stages, in theaters, nightclubs and comedy clubs. Schools, community centers, youth centers, zoos and museums also occasionally hire ventriloquists to entertain children. See https://www.theartcareerproject.com/careers/ventriloquism, retrieved March 27, 2021.

The website of the Theater Art Career Project points out that there are no strict educational requirements for a career in ventriloquism. Education and training in the performance arts, however, can help aspiring ventriloquists learn the necessary skills for a successful career, doing so as a preprofessional amateur. Those interested in a professional career in this art often have a number of options in finding the right degree program. These performing artists might want to explore degree programs in acting, drama and the theater arts. Some schools also offer degrees or workshops in comedy or ventriloquism. Finally, professional work in this art typically requires linking up with an agent.

Client-Centered Professions

For our purposes, these occupations stand out from their public-centered counterparts according to three important characteristics: extensive formal training, legally based formal certification and lack of a pure amateur career stage. Among the client-centered professions, we find physicians, lawyers, teachers, architects, chartered accountants, engineers, pharmacists, veterinarians, registered nurses and dentists. More accurately, they are known as the "liberal professions," which are, according to the European Union's Directive on Recognition of Professional Qualifications (2005/36/EC), "those practiced on the basis of relevant professional qualifications in a personal, responsible and professionally independent capacity by those providing intellectual and conceptual services in the interest of the client and the public." The adjective of "liberal" is necessary here to separate this kind of professional from the general professional or someone who is remunerated for working in an occupation whatever the nature of that work.

The road to devotee work in the client-centered professions is paved with, often lengthy, formal education, training and practicums at the preprofessional (amateur) stage. By way of such formation successful students in their pursuit are authenticated with university degrees and, for some, official licenses (e.g., law, medicine) all of which legitimate professional client-centered practice. Thus, the transition to the gainfully employment stage of devotee work is comparatively smooth, though certainly rigorous in the preprofessional years and possibly fraught with difficulties in getting established in the early years of this stage. In other words, the seeds of the amateur love for this work are sown in school, but sprout and blossom later as devotee work.

Conclusions

The foregoing pages suggest that the liberal professions, as a major type of occupation, meet the six criteria for occupational devotion. The core activities are profound; they require skill, knowledge or experience. Each profession offers significant variety to its practitioners. Furthermore, creativity and innovation are the hallmark of these kinds of work, and the devotees have reasonable control over the amount of time they put in it. Those who make the profession their life work show, at least initially, a taste and aptitude for the core activities. Nevertheless, this orientation can change over the years, as Mellor (2006) has shown for teachers and lawyers who abandoned (grew disenchanted with) their callings. Finally, the physical and social milieu in which they work is conducive to liberal professional success.

Do these criteria hold for the consulting professions? This is the subject of the next chapter.

Notes

1 This partial list of types and techniques has a Western bias and would grow significantly were we to add Asian, Middle-Eastern, and South American approaches to art.
2 The distinction between pure and preprofessional amateur is elaborated in Stebbins (1979, 36).
3 These three concepts are further discussed in Stebbins (1980).

Chapter 3

CONSULTANTS

According to Wikipedia ("Consultant," *Wikipedia*, retrieved April 5, 2021) "a consultant is usually an expert or an experienced professional in a specific field and has a wide knowledge of the subject matter. The role of consultant outside the medical sphere (where the term is used specifically for a grade of doctor) can fall under one of two general categories." One is the "internal consultant," who works in an organization and whose specialization is valued by certain internal clients, namely, other departments or individuals. The other category—the "external consultant"—who is hired on a temporary basis by a consulting firm or other agency and is paid a fee for the expertise provided. Wikipedia states that:

> Consulting firms range in size from sole proprietorships consisting of a single consultant, small businesses consisting of a small number of consultants, to mid- to large consulting firms, which in some cases are multinational corporations. This type of consultant generally engages with multiple and changing clients, which are typically companies, non-profit organizations, or governments.

The external consultant is the subject of this chapter. There are 45 types of this worker listed on the Wikipedia website, of which we will look at a representative sample of 11. In general, consultants meet, in nearly ideal fashion, the six criteria for occupational devotion. They are deeply knowledgeable and experienced in their specialty, and each opportunity to apply this background is unique. Consultants are hired to solve problems, which opens the door to creative or innovative solutions on their part. Further, they are often self-employed, acquiring thereby reasonable control over the amount and disposition of time they put into it each day. It goes without saying that, since these workers have aspired to be consultants, they have both a taste and an aptitude for the core activities. The social and physical milieu in which they must work may not always, however, be ideal. This can be a problem when they work on-site with a client, as opposed to working in their professional office.[1]

Legal Nurse Consultant

According to the American Association of Legal Nurse Consultants (AALNC), legal nurse consulting is

> the analysis and evaluation of facts and testimony and the rendering of informed opinions related to the delivery of nursing and other healthcare services and outcomes, and the nature and cause of injuries. The legal nurse consultant is a licensed registered nurse who performs a critical analysis of clinically related issues in a variety of settings in the legal arena. (AALNC: What is an LNC? Retrieved April 7, 2021)

The following list from the AALNC site shows how diverse the professional life of these consultants can be. They participate in client interviews as part of the legal team. They identify, organize and analyze pertinent medical records, from which they must often prepare a chronology, timeline or other summaries of documentation. Legal nurse consultants may also conduct medical literature searches and assist in additional research. Furthermore, they may have to identify applicable standards of care in medical malpractice cases. Concerning expert witnesses, these nurses identify, screen and facilitate review of them. In general, they may need to educate attorneys and clients regarding relevant medical issues.

Turning to the cases themselves, the legal nurse may have to evaluate case strengths and weaknesses and even draft or analyze medical portions of legal documents. This work can include evaluating causation and damage issues as well as participating in case management and case strategy discussions. Legal nurses may even serve as a nurse expert witness.

Otherwise, legal nurses as consultants identify plaintiff's future medical needs and associated costs. They also attend independent medical exams and perform cost of care estimates for long-term care treatment and catastrophic case management scenarios. Given their wide experience in the judicial arena, they are occasionally invited to do miscellaneous activities less directly related to their training as nurses, such as locate or prepare demonstrative evidence for trial or help with preparation for and support during deposition and trial.

Framed in the conceptual language of occupational devotion, legal nurse consulting can be seen as a "recreational specialization" (Bryan 1977), in particular, one occurring after several years of practice as a regular nurse (RN). With this background, legal nurses must then be certified, a recognition achieved by completing a college or university program expressly designed to train these workers. The amateur part of this career is experienced primarily, if not exclusively, in the formal instruction and practical work of nursing education, both for the RN and for the legal nurse certification.

Consulting Psychology

The American Psychological Association defines consulting psychology as:

> the function of applying and extending the specialized knowledge of a psychologist through the process of consultation to problems involving human behavior in various areas. A consulting psychologist shall be defined as a psychologist who provides specialized technical assistance to individuals or organizations in regard to the psychological aspects of their work. Such assistance is advisory in nature and the consultant has no direct responsibility for its acceptance. Consulting psychologists may have as clients individuals, institutions, agencies, corporations or other kinds of organization. (https://www.APA.org, retrieved September 12, 2021)

The object is, in general, to improve the client's efficiency and effectiveness.

The APA's Division 13 notes that, in general, a consultation begins with entry, moves through diagnosis and implementation to an ending followed by a clear disengagement. According to Wikipedia ("Consulting Psychology," *Wikipedia*, retrieved April 9, 2021), there are seven distinct types.

1. Client-centered consulting focuses on an individual client who is a recipient of service. Here, the consultant helps the service provider to better help that client. In other words, the consultant assesses the client, makes a diagnosis and recommends changes to the consultee, who is often a teacher, physician or care provider.
2. The consultee-centered consulting psychologist focuses on the consultee rather than a particular client, helping build new skills via training and/or supervision. This psychologist does not usually meet clients directly. In this type consultees seek consultation to increase their knowledge, skills, confidence and/or objectivity.
3. Consultee-centered administrative consultation centers on administrative rather than professional staff. Relationships in this type are typically longer term. Here, the practitioner becomes involved with an organization and its bureaucracy.
4. The behavioral consultation type conceives of the consultant as an expert who assumes primary responsibility for the consultative relationship. The focus is on problem solving more than on skills development or a particular

client. In other words, the larger pictures of the client as a person or the organization as a group remain in the background.

5. Organization consulting psychology uses systems theory to improve productivity or to streamline the relationship between an organization and its environment. In this case, the organization is the client. Further, this psychologist will need an interdisciplinary understanding of the client organization in the larger society.

6. The statistical consulting psychologist acts as a statistical expert who examines empirical evidence and makes sophisticated analyses by way of consulting tests and certified projects. This type must also be knowledgeable of relevant research design, sampling and qualitative methodology.

7. The litigation and risk management consulting psychologists specialize in jury thought and decision-making processes. They are usually hired to help attorneys and insurance companies evaluate the risks of lawsuits or the application of settlements, if not both.

The road to licensed consulting psychologist is long and demanding. Such serious leisure interests as volunteer mentoring (Stebbins 2006) and advising individuals or groups may generate an appetite for consultative work, but much formal (preprofessional) training lies ahead starting with obtaining a doctorate in psychology. Next aspirants must log in many supervised hours—ranging in the United States, for instance, from 1,500 to 6,000 depending on the state. After this, they must pass the Examination for Professional Practice in Psychology (EPPP). A jurisprudence exam, if applicable, also awaits them. Success at these leads to recognition by a state licensing board that requirements have been met and that they can now claim the title of licensed psychologist.

Consultant Pharmacist

A consultant pharmacist is a pharmacist who is paid to provide expert advice on the use of medications by individuals, by people within institutions or through the provision of pharmacy services to institutions. Consultant pharmacists are defined by their common commitment to enhance the quality of care for all older persons through the appropriate use of medication and promotion of healthy aging. These professionals are now practicing in a wide variety of settings outside the traditional pharmacy wherever seniors reside, including subacute care and assisted living facilities, psychiatric hospitals, hospice programs and home and community-based care (https://www.ascp.com/what-can-senior-care-pharmacist-do-you, retrieved April 11, 2021).

In their roles as medication therapy management (MTM) experts, senior care pharmacists:

- hold their patients' interest above all others;
- take responsibility for their patients' medication-related needs;
- ensure that their patients' medications are the most appropriate, the safest possible, the most effective and are used correctly; and
- identify, resolve and prevent medication-related problems.

Typically, senior care pharmacists accomplish this by means of a comprehensive consultation that provides a thorough, one-on-one review of all the patient's medications—prescription, over-the-counter, herbal and nutritional.

Nevertheless, senior care pharmacists go well beyond reviewing medications. A senior care pharmacist has studied and acquired extensive knowledge about and experience in:

- observing and properly assessing the health of seniors;
- advocating healthy living practices and disease prevention for seniors;
- recognizing and understanding diseases and conditions common in the senior population;
- identifying medication-related problems that can cause, aggravate or contribute to common geriatric problems;
- making it easier for seniors to take their medications properly by better labeling, packaging and organizing prescription drugs; and
- understanding the role of caregiver, the financial challenges that seniors may face and the importance of choosing appropriate care.

Many senior care pharmacists learn these skills after years of working with residents in nursing homes. Some practitioners also demonstrate this special knowledge and training by becoming board-certified geriatric pharmacists.

According to the U.S. Bureau of Labor Statistics, "pharmacists are required to have a Doctor of Pharmacy (Pharm.D.) degree, a postgraduate professional degree." Doctor of Pharmacy programs at most universities take three to four years to complete. In the language of devotee work, pharmacy students at the undergraduate and graduate levels are preprofessional amateurs. A pure amateur stage of this career, wherein a neophyte enthusiast learns pharmacy through self-directed learning, appears to be highly unlikely (Turner and McAlpine 2011).

Certification

The Commission for Certification in Geriatric Pharmacy (CCGP) offers a voluntary certification program for pharmacists the world over. The CCGP is a member of the Institute for Credentialing Excellence and the Council on Credentialing in Pharmacy. It is also accredited by the National Commission for Certifying Agencies (https://en.wikipedia.org/wiki/Commission for Certification in Geriatric Pharmacy).

To become certified, eligible pharmacists must pass a written examination on geriatric pharmacy practice and principles of geriatric drug therapy. The CCGP partners with a professional testing company, Applied Measurement Professionals, to ensure the examination is psychometrically valid and meets all the appropriate standards of certification. A pharmacist who passes the examination is designated as a Certified Geriatric Pharmacist (CGP).

Education Consultant

According to the Society of Education Consultants, these practitioners come from a wide range of backgrounds and experience and bring a comprehensive range of skills and knowledge:

> They include head teachers and senior leaders, Local Authority officers, inspectors and advisers. They are skilled at helping you analyse problems and find the solutions to help you move forward and understand in depth how to work with leaders and organisations to help them develop. As they spend time in many schools and organisations they are able to observe numerous examples of good, innovative practice which can be shared with your school. (https://www.sec.org.uk/What-Education-Consultants-Do, retrieved April 12, 2021)

In particular, these consultants bring their expertise and experience to bear on school and subject specialties, teaching and learning, support for school leadership and matters of inclusion. They can also shed light on personnel issues, working with others and questions of marketing. International issues and teacher training/development also fall within the purview of education consultation.

Many education consultants help parents/students and organizations with educational planning. These professionals offer similar services to school counselors, but are normally self-employed or employed by consulting firms, whereas school counselors are employed by the schools. The Higher Education Consultants Association is a US-based professional association focused exclusively on the practice of college admissions consulting, while members of the Independent Educational Consultants Association also assist students with consulting specialties that include college admission, day and boarding school, at-risk students and learning disabilities.

Specialists in this field visit numerous colleges and universities each year to learn about admissions practices and policies. Members of the professional associations hold a master's degree or higher, and many hold a bachelor's certificate in college admissions counseling. Credentialing is, at present, less universal in educational consulting compared with, for example, that in geriatric pharmacy.

Viewed from the angle of devotee work, students in this field at the undergraduate and graduate levels are preprofessional amateurs. A pure amateur stage of this career, wherein a neophyte enthusiast learns educational consulting by means of self-directed learning, would be extremely rare.

Human Resources Consultant

This consultant can fill two typical roles (Poór and Józsa 2015):

Expert Resource Consultant, who suggests solutions based on his expertise and experience, discusses with the clients the correctness of these solutions and gives assistance in the implementation. Expert consultant transfer typically tacit knowledge. This role is very typical in information—benchmarking and design consulting. Drucker [for references see Poór and Józsa 2015] called as knowledge—provider the management consultant in his publication even in a quarter century ago.

Process/People consultant, who assists the client in searching for solutions with methods that facilitate and raise creativity of the employee's clients; and therefore the clients themselves will be able to implement solutions. The root of this approach goes back to Kurt Lewin [for references see Poór and Józsa 2015]. This role has traditionally been demonstrated by organizational development and change consulting. The Process Consultant typically transfers tacit knowledge.

The following are the core fields on which most human resource consultancies are based (https://en.wikipedia.org/wiki/Human_resource_consulting, retrieved April 13, 2021):

Employee engagement: The consultant measures employee engagement levels using surveys and interviews to define and improve performance in engagement and retention.

Compensation: In this field consultants design and manage compensation programs related to basic salary, bonuses, and stock plans. They also evaluate positions and build salary structures, bonus plans, and stock plans for clients. Some consultants specialize in this area, often according to type of employee (e.g., executive compensation, sales worker compensation).

Employee benefits: Here consultants strive to optimize benefit plan design and administration (including health-related benefits), accomplished by assessing competitiveness and effectiveness of benefit plans and cost-effectiveness and the quality of vendors.

Actuarial and retirement: Consultants in this field provide actuarial and administrative services to manage cost and effectiveness of retirement programs. Their work includes defined benefit and defined contribution plans.

Mergers and acquisitions: These two events often require coordination and administration of cross-functional activities during execution, including payroll and human resource management system technology. It also falls to HR consultants to align organizational cultures and work styles in the post-merger period.

Talent mobility: In this capacity, the consultant provides the insight and execution for full international expatriates (usually for executives) or local plus (partial-package expatriates). This runs from a pre-move informative guide to a post-move expat management program.

Educational background

A bachelor's degree in human resources is commonly required and may be structured as a Bachelor of Arts (BA), Bachelor of Science (BS) or Bachelor of Business Administration (BBA). These programs prepare students to supervise a human resources personnel department in which they would oversee business, financial and legal issues related to company employees. Coursework in these programs emphasizes the management of human capital and the mastery of knowledge and skills associated with human resource planning and analysis, equal opportunity compliance, staffing, human resource development, compensation, benefits and employee and labor/management relations.

Furthermore, many human resource consultants obtain specialized qualifications or certifications in such disciplines as accountancy, actuarial science, education studies, finance, general consulting, HR consulting, health and benefits studies, compensation studies and behavioral psychology. For practicing HR consultants certifiable training in any of these specialties may also need to be sought, which involves more undergraduate education or postgraduate work.

Here, too, the serious leisure career phase of this devotee occupation is almost exclusively experienced, if not entirely so, at the preprofessional amateur level.

Information Technology Consultant

Information technology (IT) refers to the use of computers to store, retrieve, transmit and manipulate data, or information. It is typically employed in business operations as opposed to personal or entertainment technologies (http://foldoc.org/Information+Technology, retrieved April 14, 2021). Applied computer systems include both hardware and software and, often, networking and telecommunications.

In management, IT consulting is a field of activity centered on advising organizations on how best to use IT to achieve their business objectives (https://en.wikipedia.org/wiki/information_technology_consulting, retrieved April 14, 2021).

Typically, an IT consultant specializes in one key area or domain. They can consult about and help implement websites, software, network infrastructure, cloud environments, enterprise resource planning (ERP) and other related business solutions
In particular, an IT consultant helps organizations with:

- understanding and analyzing the IT requirements of the organization and the underlying environment;
- advising IT solutions and services based on requirements;
- managing and supervising the implementation process; and
- helping organizations and employees with the change management process.

An IT consultant typically works independently, even while this person may also be affiliated with an IT consultancy or professional services firm.

According to Job Hero (https://www.jobhero.com/job-description, retrieved April 14, 2021), technology consultants advise businesses on the IT that can used to support business goals and profitability. Most technology consultants have at least a bachelor's degree and skills in analysis, business strategy, marketing, problem solving, team coordination and communication.

Again, most of the impetus for a career in IT roots in its preprofessional amateur stage, in formal educational college/university programs.[2] Job Hero notes that, generally, technology consultants have at least a bachelor's degree in a related field such as IT or computer science. Many also have advanced degrees in technology or business-related fields. Additionally, most technology consultants have practical, hands-on experience with IT as system administrators or architects, IT managers or executives. Though there are few opportunities for on-the-job training in this role, technology consultants do need, through self-directed learning, to constantly stay on top of technological developments and emerging industry-specific trends to be able to provide informed guidance.

Media Consultant

Media consultants generally work in the area of public relations and thereby help manage the public image of an individual or group. Study.Com (https://study.com/articles/Media_Consultant) states that media consultant is a title used in many different career fields, among them telecommunications, sales and website design. It is also commonly used in the field of public relations. Here, media consultants offer advice to individuals and organizations that are seeking help in promoting and maintaining their public image. Duties may encompass a wide range of responsibilities, including:

• drafting press releases, news and magazine articles;
• setting up speaking engagements and preparing speeches for spokespersons;
• developing media plans and policies with executives in the organization; and
• directing public relations campaigns for a company or organization.

Media consultants for smaller companies may perform a wider array of duties from preparing promotional material to contacting key individuals. They may also offer training to executives on how to promote a public image and handle media relations.

A bachelor's degree is usually required for entry-level positions in this field, along with experience. The public relations field is integral to a media consultant's work duties. Having a bachelor's degree in communications, public relations or marketing will give one the skills for creating press releases, campaigns and media policies. In terms of occupational devotion, this training should be understood as preprofessional amateur activity, with earlier experience at the purely amateur level being highly unusual.

Political Consultant

Political consulting is a form of consulting that consists primarily of advising and assisting political campaigns. Although the most important role of political consultants is arguably the development and production of mass media (largely television and direct mail), consultants advise campaigns on many other activities, ranging from opposition research and voter polling, to field strategy and efforts to get out the vote (https://en.wikipedia.org/wiki/Politi cal Consulting).

Wise-Geek.Com defines the political consultant as a type of management consultant who focuses on the campaigns of political figures (www.wise-geek.com/what-is-a-political-consultant.htm, retrieved April 15, 2021). This person can be looked on as a sort of advertising executive, but instead of selling a tangible product or service, they are selling the idea of an individual as a candidate. These consultants exist throughout the world, and especially in the United States, they comprise a reasonably massive industry.

Political consultants sometimes act as political strategists, a senior political consultant who promotes the election of certain candidates or the interests of certain groups. This is achieved by planning campaign strategies, coordin-ating campaign staffers and arranging events to publicize candidates or causes. They can also act as public relations specialists, salespeople and managers. By using many forms of marketing-suitable media, including advertising and press releases, the general goal of political consultants is to make voters aware of their candidates' party platform.

Like the politicians, they serve these consultants work in a unique occu-pation (Stebbins 2019). There are no strict educational requirements, even though a master's or doctoral degree is common (https://study.com/articles/ Become_a_Political_Consultant_Step-by-Step_Career_Guide.html, retrieved April 15, 2021). Study.Com suggests a degree field, namely, political science, political administration or a similar field. There are no general licenses or certifications required. Strong analytical, critical-thinking and writing skills are said to be key. And this website lists additional requirements, among them, knowledge of law, government, communications and media practices and an ability to analyze election results and other political data.

In political consultation, it is quite possible that these professionals get their start as committed volunteers in political parties and campaigns. From here, they can pursue their devotee career by way of self-directed learning through relevant university and adult education courses a well as pertinent reading material. The American Association of Political Consultants, an international organization, offers various practical seminars, a code of ethics and certifica-tion in a handful of specialties.

Professional Engineering Consultant

Engineering is the branch of science and technology concerned with the design, building and use of engines, machines and structures. Consultants in this field are considered applied scientists who serve fee-paying clients and, hence, must be regulated and licensed by the state. In other words, as with many professions, the professional status and the actual practice of professional engineering is legally defined and, in some jurisdictions, protected by law.

Requirements in the United States for licensing vary, but generally are as follows:

1. Graduate from an Accreditation Board for Engineering and Technology (ABET)-accredited four-year college or university program with a degree in engineering (e.g., Bachelor of Engineering, Bachelor of Science in Engineering, Master of Science in Engineering, Master of Engineering) or in some states, graduate from an ABET-accredited four-year college or university program with a degree in engineering technology.
2. Complete a standard Fundamentals of Engineering (FE) written examination, which tests applicants on breadth of understanding of basic engineering principles and, optionally, some elements of an engineering speciality. Completion of the first two steps typically qualifies applicants for certification in the United States as an engineer in training (EIT), sometimes also called an engineer intern (EI).
3. Accumulate a certain amount of engineering experience: In most states the requirement is four years, but it is lower in some. For engineering technology graduates, the required number of years may be higher.
4. Complete a written Principles and Practice in Engineering (PE) examination, which tests the applicant's knowledge and skills in their chosen engineering discipline (civil, electrical, industrial, mechanical, etc.), as well as engineering ethics. (https://en.wikipedia.org/wiki/Regulation and licensure in engineering, retrieved April 16, 2021)

There appears to be scant opportunity to develop an interest in engineering strictly as an amateur, therefore, leaving it to emerge at the preprofessional stage of a career in devotee work.

Theater Consultant

A theatre consultant is a specialist in the design of facilities for the performing arts, equipment for those facilities and the operation of theatres. Professional consultants provide unbiased, functionally sound, practical consulting and design services for performance and public assembly facilities of all kinds (https://en.wikipedia.org/wiki/American Society of Theatre Consultants, retrieved April 17, 2021). Theatre consultants are professionals. With their vast knowledge of layouts, codes and functions of theatre and performance spaces, they are hired by a contractor, architect or owner to advise owners and design teams during the planning and building of the project. American Society of Theatre Consultants says its members must also be well versed in such technical criteria as the planning, design and equipping of theatres, concert halls and other types of facilities used for public assembly and presentation of the performing arts.

The professional organization in the United States is the American Society of Theatre Consultants. The international equivalent organization is the Institute of Theatre Consultants. Theatre consulting is not regulated by professional license, but the Institute of Theatre Consultants accredits theatre consultants on the basis of proven work, operates a Code of Practice and provides training to members.

Theatre consultants may work directly for a facility or organization, or they may be contracted as a specialty consultant for a project architect or engineer. Services can range from programmatic planning for the development of new facilities, planning for the refurbishment or repurposing of existing facilities, or just (re)design or assessment of specific production systems.

Some of these consultants have obtained BFAs or MFAs, but many seem to drift into professional consultation through accumulated experience of advising on the needs of theater and working in different sectors of this industry.[3] This amounts to a combination of self-directed learning and on-the-job training, which to the extent that the consultative activity is at best lightly remunerated, can be classified as core devotee amateurism (see Chapter 2).

Urban Planning Consultant

An urban planner develops plans and programs for the use of land. As consultants, they use planning to create communities, accommodate growth or revitalize physical facilities in towns, cities, counties and metropolitan areas.

In particular, urban planners typically do the following:

- meet with public officials, developers and the public regarding development plans and land use;
- gather and analyze economic and environmental studies, censuses, and market research data;
- conduct field investigations to analyze factors affecting land use;
- review site plans submitted by developers;
- assess the feasibility of proposals and identify needed changes;
- recommend whether proposals should be approved or denied;

- present projects to planning officials and planning commissions; and
- stay current on zoning or building codes, environmental regulations, and other legal issues. (https://www.planning.org, Offers Resources for Planning Careers)

Most urban planners have a master's degree, and the common areas of study are Urban Planning, Geography, Architecture and Environmental Science. Most also work for various levels of government, real estate developers, nonprofits and planning consulting firms. They work throughout a country in all sizes of municipality, but most work in large metropolitan areas. Furthermore, they usually work in small teams, which deliver a collective consultation.

The American Institute of Certified Planners (AICP) offers certification in urban planning, which requires the applicant to have a bachelors or master's degree in that field and two to four years of postgraduate experience. Applicants without these academic credentials may still apply, but they must have eight years of experience. The upshot of this is that serious leisure involvement in urban planning is largely confined to the preprofessional amateur variety. Still, AICP does consider applicants for certification without either relevant degree, leaving open the door for pure amateurs to seek devotee work in this field.

Conclusions

In this type of devotee work, the preprofessional amateur is a main career stage in all but political consultation, which of course, is also true for their counterparts, the liberal professionals. An as yet unknown number of political consultants start as career volunteers and subsequently find work as politicians or consultants, if not both. And, as mentioned, some theater consultants may enter this occupation through the door of core devotee participation as pure amateurs or professionals. But consultation is attractive, if for no other reason than that the worker is self-employed. It therefore meets well the fourth of the six criteria. Being one's own boss can be appealing.

Next on our tour of the devotee occupations are the skilled trades and crafts.

Notes

1   This statement on meeting the six criteria squares well with Looka's description of consulting (https://looka.com/blog/types-of-consulting, retrieved 4 April 2021).
2   It is true that many a high school youth is fascinated with computers and what they can do, which may upon research, show that this helps foster an interest in postsecondary education in IT consultation.
3   To find data supporting this observation, I studied the websites of a variety of theater consultants.

Chapter 4

SKILLED TRADES AND CRAFTS

There is a long history of the evolution of the modern skilled trades and crafts, which is well presented in a variety of sources (e.g., "Skilled Trades, History of" in *Encyclopedia Britannica*). Therefore, the present chapter centers not on this history but on those trades and crafts that meet the six criteria of occupational devotion listed in Chapter 1 and how they do this. We also look here at the hobbyist beginnings that inspire this career.

Skilled trades workers engage in activities at which they improve with experience, on-the-job training, apprenticeship and, more and more, with formal vocational training. These leisure/work participants often work manually with things, substances, liquids and the like to produce a product or a service. Formal training in a one- or two-year program commonly leads to certification in the trade, and sometimes a craft, and may be followed by apprenticeship. Some trades and crafts allow for on-the-job training.

How are trades and crafts distinguished? A common description of the latter is that they require "knowledge and skill which produces useful objects and activities [and] implies an aesthetic, standards on which judgments of particular items of work can be based" (Becker 1982, 274). In some crafts that aesthetic is innovation, finding an imaginative way to solve a practical problem (e.g., electrical, plumbing).

We will examine a reasonably representative sample consisting of 12 trades/crafts, wherein hobbyists/workers can experience occupational devotion anchored later in their careers in a small business, either their own or that of an employer. Each of the 12 will be described and assessed according to the criteria for devotee work set out earlier. We start with masonry workers.

Masonry Workers

These devotees work in brick, concrete block, stone or terrazzo. They experience the creative side of their occupation while building such structures as walls, fireplaces, floors and patios. Terrazzo workers create decorative finishes by blending fine marble chips into the epoxy, resin or cement, which is often colored. They construct decorative walkways, floors, patios and panels. There is considerable variety in masonry, evident especially in the shapes of and materials used for fireplaces and patios.

Building and masonry contractors impose time frames on the masonry workers they hire to construct fireplaces, patios and the like. The latter, however, typically work alone on these projects. Within that time frame, they therefore control their pace of work. Nonetheless, because they often work outside, they are subject to a list of disagreeable climatic conditions, among them, heat, cold, rain, wind, mud and dust. Moreover, masonry normally involves manipulating heavy tools and materials while standing, kneeling and bending for long periods. Hence, the need to make an effort to complete the project and persevere at it during its disagreeable moments.

Given the previous description of masonry, amateur masons are probably, in one sense, rare creatures; they are at most leisure-based enthusiasts limited to doing projects rather than pursuing the activity at a steady pace. In another sense, however, amateur masons exist as formal apprentices or on-the-job trainees. Here, they build their knowledge of and skill in the trade. If they continue on to work in the occupation as a livelihood, they are identifiable theoretically as occupational devotees.

Electricians and Plumbers

Electricians install, maintain and repair electrical power, communications, lighting and control systems. Most of them learn through a formal apprenticeship, although these days, many start their career by attending a technical school. Here, they gain certification, which most governments require of electricians.

The opportunity for innovation belongs mainly to electricians working in new, non-standardized structures, where they must fulfill the special needs of their clients (e.g., new homes, offices and office buildings). In older structures, innovation appears as a requirement of electrical repairs, seen in using testing devices, replacing dated or worn installations and meeting remodeling needs. The work of these participants sometimes takes place in disagreeable physical circumstances such as repairs in cramped or hard-to-reach structures and external activity in cold weather. Here, too, there is need to make an effort and persevere at it.

Most hobbyist electrical work appears to be part of a do-it-yourself (DIY) orientation toward household chores, a set of activities that may be mostly, if not entirely, of the nonwork obligation variety (Stebbins 2021). Nevertheless, some of these participants may find electrical work to be both appealing and fulfilling, enough so as to become interested in finding an occupational career in it. They therefore continue in their hobbyist mode through school and apprenticeship to become certified devotee electricians. A practitioner of 39 years in the field expressed his feelings about his career:

> If you're bored, look at other niches in the field. Everything I am is wrapped up in electrical. I pretty much do this 24/7/365. I even take my hand tools on vacation so I can fix family electrical problems. I have a hard time relating [to boredom]. Maybe it's because I work on everything except medical/hospital wiring. One day I will be roughing a house, the next troubleshooting a waste water treatment plant, or wiring a gas station, or designing a solar system. There's so much to do and learn. (*Electrician Talk*, June 26, 2017, https://www.electriciantalk.com/threads/do-you-like-being-an-electrician.212962, retrieved November 28, 2020).

Plumbers

Plumbers are included in the electrician case because they work in similar conditions. They install pipes and fixtures, inspect and test installed pipe systems and pipelines, troubleshoot malfunctioning systems and maintain and repair plumbing systems. Troubleshooting, maintenance and repair are the principal activities lending themselves to innovation in this occupation.

Plumbers must also meet the special needs of their clients presenting new, non-standardized structures (e.g., new homes, offices and office buildings). They, too, sometimes work in older structures, where innovation appears as a requirement of plumbing repairs, evident in replacing dated or worn installations and meeting remodeling needs. Furthermore, the work of these participants sometimes takes place in disagreeable physical circumstances such as repairs in cramped or hard-to-reach structures and external activity in cold weather. Here there is also need to make an effort and persevere at it.

The early career line of plumbers is also similar to that of electricians. Rarely, it appears, does plumbing as a leisure interest get ignited as positive DIY. More commonly some of these participants somehow find plumbing to be both appealing and potentially fulfilling, enough so as to become interested in seeking an occupational career in it. They therefore continue in their hobbyist mode through trade school and apprenticeship to get certified as devotee plumbers.

Brewers and Microbrewing

Home brewing is a multistep process using such ingredients as grain (often barley) to create an alcoholic beverage. The hobbyist brewer is aided by commercially available kits for beginning and advanced participants. Most kits come with a full set of instructions for brewing. All-grain kits include all the ingredients needed to create homebrewed beer. These kits usually include grain and hops, and some may include yeast. A full set of instructions is normally enclosed.

What is innovative about this hobby? David Ackley (2019) writes that

> there is an art to homebrewing—a creativity, but creativity isn't just haphazardly throwing in whatever ingredients come to mind. The art is in understanding balance. How much hop bitterness is appropriate for a Bohemian pilsner? How much *coriander* should be used in a Belgian wit? One could easily follow a recipe, but a true artist will know from experience when enough is enough.

> And, of course, there's an art to the act of brewing. There's a certain art to learning how and when to transfer beer from one fermenter to another, and a certain art to bottling without losing a drop of beer. Again, the art is improved with experience.

Thurnell-Read (2016) and Alonso et al. (2017) describe the fulfilling aspects of home brewing as serious leisure. Furthermore, some of the interviewees in the Alonso et al. study expressed an interest in opening in the future a microbrewery and moving thereby into devotee work.

The Thompson Island Brewing Company (located in Delaware) distinguishes microbreweries and craft breweries.

> Where do microbreweries fit into all of this? The microbrewery definition is simple. A microbrewery makes less than 15,000 barrels of beer each year, and 75% or more of it must be served off-site. The term is unfortunately unclear to many, with people often using "microbrewery" to refer to any business that brews craft beer. The only difference between a craft brewery and a microbrewery is volume. A craft brewery doesn't necessarily indicate a microbrewery, although many microbreweries do brew craft beer. Likewise, a microbrewery does still have to meet craft brewing standards to be a craft brewery. (Thompson Island Brewing Company 2019, retrieved December 26, 2020).

The craft brewers are small, independent businesses, operating without substantial guidance from any non-craft brewer. Their hallmark is innovation. Craft brews are made with traditional ingredients as a base, often with added nontraditional ingredients to provide distinction.

Hobbyist Cooks

Hobbyist cooks are gourmet cooks, not the everyday kitchen drudges whose nonwork obligations include getting food on the table for self and family. Jenna Hartel (2003, 2007) has studied the hobbyist cooks, as hobby is defined in the Serious Leisure Perspective (SLP). She explored their information activities, resources and spaces used in their gourmet cooking, undertaken sufficiently often and regularly to qualify as a hobby.

Gourmet cooking allows for considerable innovation. Thus, recipes dictate ingredients and cooking methods, but these cooks may experiment with both. Moreover, since they are preparing a meal, they must present it in appetizing ways, including all elements of it. That is, side dishes must complement the main course, including the dessert. Such considerations also rest on the innovative talents of the participant.

It is not known if and how often hobbyist cooks seek a professional career as devotee chefs. The modern chef working in a restaurant serving what qualifies as gourmet cuisine commonly has considerable formal training. Chefs can be formally trained at an institution, followed by an apprenticeship with an experienced chef. Alternatively, some get trained through an extensive apprenticeship arrangement. Culinary institutions offer diploma, associate and bachelor's degree programs in the culinary arts. Depending on the level of education, these can take one to four years to complete. An internship is often part of such training program. Regardless of the level of education received, most professional kitchens are based on the apprenticeship system, and most new cooks start at a lower-level second or first cook position and work their way up in the ranking system.

Additionally, expert chefs must develop a knowledge of food science, nutrition and diet, while also being responsible for preparing and serving meals that are both pleasing to the eye and attractive to the palate. Hobbyists cooks share these aesthetic criteria with their restaurant counterparts, but they typically lack the technical knowledge of food science and the like. Nor do the hobbyists have to face the commercial forces that the chefs do, which are to create menus of sufficient variety and quality to retain a clientele large enough to keep the restaurant in business. In short, it seems unlikely that an occupational devotee career path will develop that leads from hobbyist gourmet cook to professional chef.

Metalworkers

Wikipedia defines metalworking as

> the process of working with metals to create individual parts, assemblies, or large-scale structures. The term covers a wide range of work

from large ships and bridges to precise engine parts and delicate jewelry. It therefore includes a correspondingly wide range of skills, processes, and tools. Metalworking is a science, art, hobby, industry and trade. ("Metalworking," *Wikipedia*, retrieved December 3, 2020).

Hobbyist metalworkers typically pursue this passion in their basement or garage. Compared with their industrial counterparts, the output of the former is small-scale and may be practical such as knives, hammers, external flower boxes and wind chimes. Artistic work is evident in jewelry, wall hangings, vases and sculptures. Most of the tools used here are hand-held, including ball peen hammer, tin snips, scratch awl, steel square, vise and hack saw. (For additional examples, see https://www.hobbies-and-pastimes.com/metal-working.html.)

Industrial sheet metal workers, by contrast, commonly work on much bigger projects. They fabricate or install products made from thin metal sheets. According to the *Occupational Outlook Handbook* (U.S. Bureau of Labor Statistics) sheet metal workers typically do the following:

- Select types of sheet metal according to building or design plans
- Measure and mark dimensions and reference lines on metal sheets
- Drill holes in metal for screws, bolts and rivets
- Install metal sheets with supportive frameworks
- Fabricate or alter parts at construction sites
- Maneuver and anchor large sheet metal parts
- Fasten seams or joints by welding, bolting, riveting or soldering

These workers use pieces of thin steel, aluminum or other alloyed metal in manufacturing and construction sites. The products of their labor include heating and air conditioning ducts, rain gutters, outdoor signs and siding.

Occasions for innovative industrial sheet metal work are similar to those of electricians and plumbers: available in work in new, non-standardized structures where they must meet the special needs of their clients (e.g., new homes, offices and office buildings). Industrial sheet metal workers often have to lift heavy materials and stand for long periods of time. As installers of sheet metal, they must often bend, climb and squat. Most of them work full time. Sheet metal workers employed in construction typically learn their trade through an apprenticeship. Thus, those employed in industry typically learn on the job often these days with some technical school training.

There appears to be little or no career leading from hobbyist metalworkers to their closest equivalent in industry: the industrial sheet metal worker. A main reason for this disjunction is the stark dissimilarity between the core activities of the two types. Both find fulfilling rewards in their serious pursuit of working with metal, but do so in very different ways. Metal work is a serious pursuit, but as with cooking, its leisure side seldom seems to lead to a livelihood made possible by that passion.

Gunsmithing

Wikipedia states that a gunsmith is someone who

> repairs, modifies, designs, or builds guns. The occupation differs from an armorer, who usually replaces only worn parts in standard firearms. Gunsmiths do modifications and changes to a firearm that may require a very high level of craftsmanship, requiring the skills of a top-level machinist, a very skilled woodworker, and even an engineer. Gunsmiths perform factory-level repairs and renovations to restore […] well-used or deteriorated firearms to new condition. They may make alterations to adapt sporting guns to better fit the individual shooter that may require extensive modifications to the firearm's stocks and metal parts. Repairs and redesigns may require fabrication and fitting of unavailable parts and assemblies constructed by smiths themselves. Gunsmiths may also renew metal finishes or apply decorative carvings, or engravings to guns. Many gun shops offer smithing service on the premises (Gunsmith 2020).

Gunsmiths function as amateurs or professionals, though all appear to start as *amators* of guns also used for hunting, target sport, collecting and other interests. For some, depending on the country, guns may also be a means of personal protection. In any case, using a gun eventually requires maintenance, repair, perhaps some redesign, thereby leading the owner to DIY smithing or to a professional gunsmith. The love for guns gets amplified with this new DIY activity. And it may be augmented by taking an adult education course in the basics of it.

Making a living (full- or part-time) becomes possible when the amateur gunsmith gets enough work or this person finds sufficient employment in a small or medium-sized gunsmithing business. Some of these commercial outfits require trade school certification in the field. Either way, a clear career line exists from serious leisure to devotee work in this field, though only in societies having a rich gun culture. The United States has such a culture, which is considered unique among developed countries, as measured by the large number of firearms owned by civilians and the generally permissive regulations bearing on their use (Fisher 2012).

Calligraphy

Ruth Barbour (2020) defines calligraphy as

> the art of beautiful handwriting. The term may derive from the Greek words for "beauty" (*kallos*) and "to write" (*graphein*). It implies a sure knowledge of the correct form of letters—i.e., the conventional signs by which language can be communicated—and the skill to make them with such ordering of the various parts and harmony of proportions that the experienced, knowledgeable eye will recognize such composition as a work of art. Calligraphic work, as art, need not be legible in the usual sense of the word.

Calligraphers are amateur or professional artists who specialize in handwriting. The elegant handwriting and designs on a wedding invitation or similar special announcement are sometimes the work of a professional calligrapher (Study.Com 2020). A calligrapher designs and applies artistic lettering for many mediums using a variety of inks and other materials. Professional calligraphers are often self-employed and work as freelancers, though they also might work for a calligraphy studio. Freelance artists often face keen competition for assignments. While no degree is required for this career, formal training in adult education courses can prepare these devotees to make a living from this craft.

And a craft it is. This definition also implies that there is a client for whom the crafts person creates the useful objects or engages in the useful activities and, if professional, gets paid in some way for this effort.

The typical neophyte calligrapher is probably a self-directed learner. Such enthusiasts can avail themselves of a great range of manuals for beginners (see Amazon.com/books) and local art supplies stores that sell calligraphy pens, brushes, paper, books and the like. As these practitioners develop, they may get requests for decorating such items as wedding and event invitations, announcements and memorial documents. To the extent that these amateurs get paid for their artistic efforts, they may evolve into a part- or full-time livelihood and devotee work. Formal courses along the way might be needed to augment the participant's skill and knowledge of the art.

Furniture Making

According to the *Occupational Outlook Handbook*, "furniture makers cut, sand, join, and finish wood and other materials to make handcrafted furnishings" (Bureau of Labor Statistics, U.S. Department of Labor 2020). These occupational devotees may also do wood turning (using a lathe), wood carving and wood inlay. As hobbyists, they commonly work at home making tables, chairs, desks, cabinets, stools, among other items. They become expert in finishing them and using glue where called for in the design. They cut, sand, join and finish wood and other materials to make these handcrafted furnishings, using such tools as saws, planes, drills, squares, sanders and chisels. They are also adept at finishing their creations with varnish, paint, stain and, possibly, inlays.

In their serious leisure, these crafters make furniture for themselves and family and friends. These items are normally presented as gifts, but as their reputations expand, they may get paid for furniture made on request by admirers of their work. Hobbyist woodworkers may also be remunerated for repairing or refinishing older furniture.

The career leading to devotee work as a part- or full-time livelihood appears often to unfold gradually. Some of these participants eventually realize that they can make furniture for which some people in town are willing to pay. Such a clientele grows from, for instance, word of mouth and maker-organized displays of one's work at furniture club shows, custom (handmade) furniture stores, craft fairs and internet sites.

Indeed, hobbyist makers may (now as devotee workers) open their own retail furniture business in which they sell custom-built items, some of which are constructed according to clients' needs and specifications. This is probably a common development in many populous urban centers in the West. Consider this example from the Canadian city of Calgary:

> Ever since their first collaborative effort as students in a Geography class at McGill University [Montreal], Talar and Jean-Claude have enjoyed working together. Upon their arrival in Calgary in 1981 they both found work in a drafting firm serving the energy sector. When the difficult economic conditions of that period necessitated a career change, it seemed like the perfect opportunity to pursue self-employment in the crafts, an area that had always held their interest. Making furniture was the ideal choice as they could combine Jean-Claude's ability in woodworking and Talar's passion for drawing and design. They started making pieces that could fulfill both an aesthetic and practical function. (source: http://www.prefontainefurniture.ca, retrieved December 12, 2020)

Nonetheless, hobbyists have always been at the vanguard of furniture development:

Necessity invented stools,
Convenience next suggested elbow-chairs,
And Luxury the accomplish'd Sofa last.
  • William Cowper, *The Task* (1785), Book I, line 86.

(taken from Wikiquote)

Quilting

Quilting is "the process of sewing the three quilt layers together, using stitches in decorative patterns as motifs, or in utilitarian patterns, such as straight lines with bigger stitches. Quilting is generally done by hand or machine" (National Quilter's Circle 2020). Participants pass an array of stitches through all layers of the fabric to construct a three-dimensional padded surface. The three layers are typically called the top fabric, or quilt top, the batting, or insulating material, and the backing.

Quilting varies from a purely functional fabric joinery technique to highly elaborate, decorative three-dimensional surface treatments. The result of the first is such utilitarian objects as bed coverings (quilts), household upholstery and items of apparel. The second is expressed mainly in wall hangings, table decorations and art objects. Nevertheless, functional quilting may also be decorative having its own aesthetic merit. And quilts can aid activist causes to the extent they bear on a social or cultural grievance. Patricia Brown (2020) discusses (with illustrative photos) the quilts that give expression to the Black Lives Matter movement in the United States.

Most quilters are hobbyists, some of whom are members of local quilting or, more broadly, craft clubs (those devoted exclusively to quilting are often called guilds). They may also join national organizations such as the Canadian Quilters Association. The serious leisure nature of this craft has been explored by, among others, King (2001) and Stalp (2006, 2007).

Professional quilters make and sell quilts sometimes doing so on commission. They may also design them, teach the art in adult education courses and present lectures (Stalp and Conti 2011). The number of pros in this field vis-à-vis hobbyists is unknown. Nor do we know how influential the former are as models for the latter. The significant influence of professionals in art, science, sport and entertainment on amateurs in these fields must be evident in a hobby to justify reconceptualizing it as an amateur art activity.

Ceramic Art

Ceramics is the art and science of making objects from inorganic, nonmetallic materials by the action of heat. It excludes glass and mosaic made from glass *tesserae*. We cover here only the studio manifestation of ceramic art, omitting thus its factory counterpart. It is the former that shows most clearly the amateur/professional link leading to devotee work.

These artistic objects are made from ceramic materials, often from clay. They take various forms, among them, artistic pottery, tableware, tiles and figurines. Some ceramics are considered fine art presented as pottery or sculpture, whereas others are more functional being designed as decorative, industrial or applied art objects [...]. Ceramic art can be made by one person or by a group of people. In a pottery or ceramic factory, a group of people design, manufacture and decorate the art ware. Products from a pottery [studio] are sometimes referred to as "art pottery." In a one-person pottery studio, ceramists or potters produce studio pottery. ("Ceramic Art," *Wikipedia*, retrieved December 19, 2020).

Studio pottery is produced by professional and amateur artists working alone or in small groups making unique items or short runs of them. Typically, all the stages of manufacture are carried out by the artists themselves (Cooper 2000). Studio pottery includes functional pieces, such as tableware and cookware, and nonfunctional ones such as ceramic sculpture. Studio potters are sometimes referred to as ceramic artists or ceramists.

Many of today's professionals have university degrees (often in art and design). They display and occasionally sell their pottery at art festivals and open houses (the whole house, not just their studio within), and over the internet (websites). They also display at craft fairs and arts complexes established for visual artists in the local community. Some operate out of a loft, typically a converted heritage building or former industrial or warehouse space. Such places commonly have exposed heating ducts, beams, concrete and brick as well as open floor plans and large windows (visual artists need ample natural light). As with the professional quilters, some ceramists must make ends by also teaching their art in adult education courses and presenting lectures. Moreover, many of them, to make ends meet, need to work a second job outside the arts or find a spouse or partner whose income is sufficient to support both of them.

Floral Designer

A professional florist describes the preprofessional life of the hobbyist in this activity:

For the hobbyist playing with flowers is grand fun. And it should be! Gather your flowers, arrange them as you like and enjoy! If you want to explore design, learn how to make the flowers last longer and expand your artistic style, we [Floral Design Institute] have Free Online Videos, and DVD's just for you. Visit the Farmers Market, visit the grocery and plant a cutting garden. The world of flowers is yours to enjoy. No, you won't be able to make a living as a florist with the perspective of a hobbyist but, you will have lots of fun!

(from Leanne's Blog, https://www.floraldesigninstitute.com/leannes-blog, retrieved December 22, 2020).

To become an occupational devotee in this field, Leanne suggests a change in orientation, notably, caring for flowers to preserve their longevity and stability of design. This means experimenting with a variety of blooms, consisting of buying flowers, taking them home and studying them there. The aspiring devotee should also take some floral design courses, which are available in certain postsecondary adult education programs. It is also necessary to build a skill library and engage in some self-directed education on working with the floral medium. The aim in all this, for the devotee, is to prepare for validation as a Floral Design Institute Certified Floral Designer and thus open the door to a livelihood in the world of flowers.

The professional florist is fully competent in a variety of design styles. The ultimate goal of many professional florists is validation with the title, Accredited in Floral Design gained through the American Institute of Floral Designers (AIFD). While both certified floral designers and accredited members of AIFD are recognized for their design abilities, AIFD members are distinguished as design artists who have committed themselves to advancing the art of professional floral design through education, service and leadership. Both AIFD and certified floral designers must maintain their status by earning continuing education units. The Floral Design Institute lists over a dozen "notable" contemporary floral designers ("Floral Design," *Wikipedia*, retrieved December 22, 2020).

The last three devotee occupations—quilting, ceramics and floral design—raise questions about their preprofessional status as amateur or hobbyist. Some of the pros are conceivably artists whose achievements serve as models to emulate for the leisure enthusiast in the activity, just as certain professionals do for amateurs.

Conclusions

The artistic devotee occupations that give rise to a small business are of the craft variety. As stated in the introduction to this chapter, they require knowledge and skill that produce useful objects and activities and imply an aesthetic. That aesthetic is one of creative beauty, exemplified earlier in the work of calligraphers, quilters, ceramicists and floral designers. The others, referred to here as trades, are sometimes practiced with an innovative aesthetic (i.e., masons, electricians, plumbers, brewers, metalworkers, cooks, gunsmiths and furniture makers).

These trades and crafts have been classified in the SLP as hobbies. Meanwhile, the arts, found under the heading of amateurs, include those devoted to the visual pursuits of painting, sculpting and photography. A critical difference separating these arts from their cousins, the crafts, is the utility of the latter. In them, practitioners (hobbyists/small business people) can make a modest living doing what they love while offering a useful product or service. Amateur/professional artists like painters and sculptors can do the same and often at a higher rate of remuneration. According to the *Occupational Outlook Handbook* (Bureau of Labor Statistics 2020), fine artists earn an annual average of USD$50,550, whereas craft artists average annually USD$34,710. Nevertheless, the amateurs and pros in the arts are primarily interested in the aesthetic side of their passion, with utility, if there is any, being secondary.

In other words, those pursuing a craft as a livelihood (full- or part-time) must build a reputation by promoting themselves and their art and selling their product or service. They often analyze the market for their crafts or art-work to increase their understanding of what prospective customers might want. Craft and fine artists may also sell their work on the internet. Thus, business acumen such as bookkeeping and marketing are valuable practical assets for these kinds of devotee workers.

Chapter 5

SMALL BUSINESSES

Perusal of the internet turned up a fair variety of devotee occupations pursued as small businesses—occupations I have placed in one of eleven categories. This typology should be taken as provisional rather than definitive. For at this, the exploratory stage in the study of occupational devotion, we should expect it to be modified in various ways as suggested by future open-ended research.

Devotee Small Businesses

Some *skilled crafts* (covered as a type of devotee work in Chapter 4) are also capable of generating devotee small businesses. Applying the six defining criteria, the work of the handyman, people who remodel homes (internally or externally), and the stonemason qualify as three examples. The handyman and those who remodel homes encounter with each project they take on some novelty and need to be innovative, as shown in research on the first (Brayham 2015; Hilbert 1994).

Plumbers, electricians and furniture makers, all examined in the preceding chapter can, in some cases, also be analyzed as owners of small devotee businesses. The main difference is that the latter typically employs a small number of other plumbers, electricians and so on who share the enthusiasm of the entrepreneur. Nevertheless, as the number of devotee workers grows, the organization tends to bureaucratize, diluting thereby, the entrepreneur's love for the job. At the beginning, these businesses must learn, usually through some kind of formal training like adult education and self-directed reading, how to run an enterprise and market their service.

Teaching as a small business is distinct from professional teaching in primary and secondary schools and institutions of higher education. It also differs from teaching the occasional adult or continuing education course, something usually done as a sideline. Rather, teaching as a small business centers on instruction of a practical kind, the demand for which is sufficient to constitute a livelihood for an instructor or small set of instructors. Thus, small businesses have been established to teach people how to ride horses, fly small airplanes and descend to earth in a parachute. Many local dance studios fall into this category, as do driver training schools, yoga studios and personal fitness programs. Innovativeness here revolves around adapting lessons to the needs of individual students and their capacities to learn the material of the course.

These instructional entities emerge to foster the self-development of their clients, often as related to a hobby for the latter. Still, driver's training and personal fitness sessions, for example, offer practical knowledge and skills largely free of hobbyist interest. However, other interests such as language acquisition and obtaining cooking and baking knowledge and skills are both practical and hobbyist. That is, the second offer the six qualities of serious leisure while meeting the criteria of devotee work. These instructors were first hobbyist equestrians, pilots or parachutists, for example, before they embarked on the entrepreneurial phase of their leisure career.

Custom work is another type of small business where occupational devotion abounds. Indeed, compared with other small business fields, it may offer the most fertile soil for this kind of personal growth. Here, to meet the wants of individual customers, the devotee designs (in collaboration with the customer) and sometimes constructs distinctive and personalized new products. Examples include workers who make their living designing and assembling on order special floral arrangements (e.g., bouquets, centerpieces) or gift baskets or confecting such as delicacies as specialty cakes, cookies and chocolates. Tailors, tattooists (Atkinson 2003), hair stylists, makeup artists and furniture makers (Jackson 2020), when working to the specifications of individual customers, also belong in this category. Alternatively, individual customers may be seeking a reshaping or remodeling of something they already possess, such as custom modifications to a car or truck or an item of apparel.

Many hair stylists and makeup artists appear to get started as amateurs who have developed a passion for such activities. Though we lack leisure research in this area, they probably gain experience and knowledge in high school drama projects, by way of self-directed reading, and possibly through personal advice from a more experienced participant. Nonetheless, remunerative work in this area requires formal preprofessional training, such as that offered for "global makeup" by Vancouver's Blanche Macdonald Centre:

1-Year Diploma Program | 920 hours | 3 days/week

Canada's most comprehensive and extensive Makeup program. Learn every facet and technique in makeup—from beauty, bridal, fashion and airbrushing to cosmetic retailing, TV & Film, special effects and prosthetics—an incredible curriculum for those aspiring to break into Hollywood North and beyond.

(https://www.blanchemacdonald.com/landing/
pro-makeup, retrieved April 29, 2021)

In general, many of these business activities are founded on a modicum of external training, such as an adult education course or two or on-the-job training with an established expert, if not both.[1] For example, a woman who likes flowers and plants finds employment in sales in a floral shop, and then, as she watches the owner create special floral arrangements, becomes interested in this activity. Furniture makers may get their inspiration from a relative whom they have observed in action. Self-directed learning can play a role here, as in reading manuals and magazines or perusing equivalent material online.

Animal work, though less prevalent than custom work and possibly even less so than devotee handicraft, nevertheless sometimes meets the seven criteria of devotee small business. The main examples here, of which I am aware, are the people who make a living training or showing, cats, dogs or horses. Just how passionately this work can be pursued is seen in Baldwin and Norris's (1999) study of hobbyist dog trainers (see also Gillespie et al. 2002; Hultsman 2015).

The only other types of animal on which we have leisure-related data is the raising and training of horses (Chevalier et al. 2011; Dashper et al. 2020) and the showing of cats (Stone 2019). From the standpoint of leisure, the animal-human link is under-researched, especially with respect to cats and horses. Concerning dogs and cats as the focus of devotee work, we lack, for example, studies of commercial dog walkers and dog and cat sitters.

Evidence that *dealers in collectibles* can be occupational devotees also comes from the field of leisure studies, where the love for collecting has been sporadically documented (e.g., Le Fur 2021; Olmsted 1991). Dealers and collectors work with such items as rare coins (Case 2009), books, stamps (Stebbins 2004c), sports cards, paintings and antiques. Still, dealers are not collectors in that their collections, if they have any, are not for sale. But even though dealers acquire collectables, they hope to sell for extrinsic speculation and profit, they, like pure collectors, also genuinely know and appreciate their many different intrinsic qualities. Thus, when such collectors face the opportunity to sell at significant profit items integral to their collections (again, if they have one), these motives may clash, causing significant personal tension (Stebbins 2004c). Here is an instance of a work-related cost that is quite capable of diluting occupational devotion.

Repair and restoration center on bringing back an item to its original state. Things in need of repair or restoration and, in the course of doing so, capable of engendering occupational devotion include old clocks and antique furniture as well as fine glass, china and crockery. There is also a business in restoring paintings and repairing musical instruments. This work, which calls for considerable skill, knowledge and experience, is typically done for individual customers. It offers great variety and opportunity for creativity and innovation.

Much of this occupation falls under the rubric of "cultural heritage" (UNESCO, http://www.unesco.org), some of which is tangible and movable (e.g., paintings, sculptures, ceramics, coins, manuscripts). Immovable tangible cultural heritage includes monuments, archaeological sites and such underwater sites as shipwrecks, ruins and even whole cities. Thus, the University of Amsterdam offers a master's degree in the conservation and restoration of cultural heritage, it being a two-year program that marks the first step to becoming a fully qualified conservator. Following the master's, one can transition into a two-year advanced professional program to work in a conservation studio and complete one or more internships to achieve the international level required to work as an independent professional conservator in a field of specialization. This does not yet qualify the student as a conservator. For this, one must successfully complete the Advanced Professional Program.

There is considerable skill and knowledge to be gained in this preprofessional amateur stage. This pursuit is fired by a passion for cultural artefacts, one possibly nurtured by family or school art courses, if not both. Once on the job, the core activities of a conservator are minimally bureaucratized.

The *service occupations* cover a huge area, though only a very small number seem to have the qualities that can generate occupational devotion. One category with this potential can be labeled "research services." Though most research is conducted by professionals, nonprofessionals do exist in certain fields. Careers leading to devotee work in the latter are evident among some hobbyist genealogists (Hershkovitz and Hardof-Jaffe 2017) and private investigators concerned with such matters as fraud, crime and civil disputes as well as industrial disputes, marital wrangles and missing persons.[2]

According to Andrea Mara (2020), successful private investigators have the following skills:

- effective communication
- computer proficiency
- sound knowledge of the law
- photography
- personal organization, including agency
- thoroughness in investigative work
- patience

Additionally, the would-be occupational devotees in this field must meet certain requirements such as those set out by California (https://www.bsis. ca.gov/forms_pubs/pi_fact.shtml, retrieved May 27, 2021). They must

> have at least three years (2,000 hours each year, totaling 6,000 hours) of compensated experience in investigative work;
>
> **or**
>
> have a law degree or completed a four-year course in police science plus two years (4,000 hours) of experience;
>
> **or**
>
> have an associate degree in police science, criminal law, or justice and 2 ½ years (5,000 hours) of experience. Experience must be certified by your employer and have been received while you were employed as a sworn law enforcement officer, military police officer, insurance adjuster, employee of a licensed PI [private investigator] or licensed repossessor, arson investigator for a public fire suppression agency, or an investigator for the public defender's office. (Work as a process server, public records researcher, custodial attendant for a law enforcement agency, bailiff, agent who collects debts in writing or by telephone after the debtor has been located, or person who repossesses property after it has been located is not considered qualifying experience.) Successful academic work, passing an examination, and other training programs lead to the Professional Investigator License.

Mara also notes that, today, some amateur sleuths have changed. They "are using genealogy databases to help solve other mysteries, with one true crime podcast, The Murder Squad, actively encouraging listeners to upload DNA profiles to GEDMatch in a bid to catch criminals." This, even though she believes that most are really, in Serious Leisure Perspective (SLP) terms, liberal arts hobbyists attracted to "discussing a news story, or watching a true crime series, or listening to a podcast, or reading crime fiction and trying to figure out whodunnit." Whether the new amateur investigator has become a remunerated occupational devotee is a question begging research.

The accident reconstruction expert also fits in the service category. Day care and dating services as well as the small *haute cuisine* restaurant and the small fund-raising enterprise constitute four other services that can generate occupational devotion, as the earlier examples suggest. And here is the classificatory location of such small business, nonprofessional consultants as those in fashion, landscaping, advertising and the emergent field of personal coaching. By and large, however, the service sector is not the place to look for exciting, fulfilling work, in part because the service itself is often banal, even if important, and in part because of the ever-present possibility of fractious customer relations.

The *artistic crafts* offer substantial scope for the would-be occupational devotee. Some are highly specialized, like etching and engraving glass, brass, wood and marble. Others are more general, including ceramics work and making jewelry. Many people in the artistic crafts are hobbyists, who earn little or no money, whereas other people try to derive some sort of living from them. It is this second group, which consists of many part-time and a few full-time workers, who may become devotees. Variety and creativity are the principal defining criteria separating them from non-devotees in this field. It is one thing to turn a dozen identical pots and quite another to turn a dozen each of which is artistically unique. Those whose sole livelihood comes from the latter are likely to be card-carrying members of the starving artist class; in a world dominated by philistines, sales of artistically different products are relatively infrequent.

The howtostartanllc.com website offers detailed advice on do-it-yourself (DIY) for-profit entrepreneurships covering more than 20 crafts along with technical legal and practical information on getting started in each as well as setting up a limited liability company in every state in the United States (How to Start an LLC, https://howtostartanllc.com/business-ideas/categor ies/craft-business-ideas).

Jourdain and Naulin (2020, 61–62) explore the innerworkings of craft marketing in the modern era:

> First, there is the revival of arts and crafts and do-it-yourself (DIY) activities driven by dedicated TV shows (like "MasterChef"), the publication of books and magazines (such as "Mollie Makes"), and the emergence of specialist shops. The second factor is the enabling role of Internet technologies giving people a way to easily sell their products and services [including] digital communication, [which] extends the possibilities for own-account working.

The authors also discuss Etsy, the online marketing service for craft workers and collectors. It is a global online marketplace, where people come together to make, sell, buy and collect unique items (Etsy, https://www.etsy.com).

Most *product marketing* is the province of organizationally based employees, working in large bureaucracies and constrained there by all sorts of rules and regulations while being locked into rigid times demands not of their making. Still, some businesses exist in this field that offer some product marketers within it a devotee occupation. The archetypical example here is the advertising agency "creative" who invents the written, audio and visual copy that helps sell a product. Evidence of this person's occupational devotion is presented by Hackley and Kover (2007, 70) who said of their sample of interviewees that

> we should not overstate the contra-organisational behaviour of creatives. They are astute enough to exploit the contradictory values of creative and business cultures to forge a professional presence in a ruthless and competitive game. Judging from our interviews, creatives appear committed to and passionate about their work.

Website design and promotion services can also be conceived of as a type of product marketing. Only two defining criteria appear to separate product marketers in small and large firms, namely, control of time and a bureaucratic milieu. These two are nonetheless salient enough to distinguish devotees from non-devotees in this area of work.

Most *planning* work is similarly bureaucratized as seen in either governmental or medium-sized business firms. Indeed, city and town planners were listed earlier as professionals. But there are others facets to the occupation of planning that, on the small business level, can generate deep occupational devotion. Here, for instance, is the classificatory home of party and event planners, who if they seek sufficient variety, meet all six defining criteria. One Achilles heel in this business is the level of efficiency of the work team, which if it fails in any major way, could result in disaster for the planner and a concomitant drop in that person's sense of occupational devotion. Thus, it is one thing to plan well for some entertainment during the conference and quite another for the entertainers to fail to show up. Funeral planners suffer similar contingencies, by far the worst being a fumbled casket during the ceremony (Habenstein 1962, 242), while in this line of work, job satisfaction and self-actualization may not typically be high enough to help generate a sense of occupational devotion (Schell and Zinger 1985).

Early stints of planning, say, for a wedding, major birthday party, or fundraising event may give the hobbyist planner a taste for such activity pursued as a livelihood. Careerexplorer.com presents a detailed discussion of event planning and education leading to a postsecondary degree that provides professional credentials (https://www.careerexplorer.com/careers/event-planner/#steps-to-becoming-an-event-planner, retrieved May 26, 2021). In the United States, they come with three educational programs offered at a small number of institutions: certificate, two-year associate degree and four-year bachelor's degree. Instruction revolves around nature of planning and duties of planners, site selection, transportation and lodging associated with the event, event registration, food and beverage management, hotel sales and operations, special event planning, nonprofit event planning, budgeting for event planners and event production software.

Careerexplorer.com conducted a survey among its members to determine their level of happiness with event planning as a career. They found that this occupation "ranks highly among careers. Overall, they rank in the 73rd percentile of careers for satisfaction scores, [though] please note that this number is derived from the data we have collected from our Sokanu members only. Despite the inherent stress of event planning, it is undeniably stimulating, exciting, even exhilarating—characteristics that define many *happy* careers." Such activity thus seems likely to become devotee work for at least some of its enthusiasts.

The *family farm* is the final small business considered here. A dwindling phenomenon, to be sure, it still nonetheless offers many owner-families an occupation to which they can become deeply attached (Farmer 2012). Though they may exploit either plants or animals, the operation must be manageable for the family. All criteria apply here, though some need explaining. Farmers must be innovative when it comes to dealing with untoward pests, weather conditions, government policies and the like. As for variety they experience it in rotating crops over the years and in observing how each crop grows during a given season. Especially at harvest time, farmers can lack control of their own hours and days. But there is usually a lengthy period between growing seasons when farmers can better direct their own lives. To the extent the farm is also run with hired hands, their level of effectiveness can contribute to or detract from the owner's level of occupational devotion.

Farmer (2012) explained how occupational devotees in farming meet the six qualities that define the serious pursuits:

> de Lauwere et al. (2004) found that farmers believe perseverance and dealing with uncertainty (e.g., weather, pests, blight) to be key personal characteristics, particularly in sustainable farming where farmers often make a career out of the experience but not necessarily their sole occupation (Salamon et al. 1997). Additionally, substantial individual effort—mental, physical, and emotional—is exerted in farming, successful or not (Arenas 2008). Durable benefits, such as "feelings of accomplishment," "social interaction and belongingness" and "physical byproducts" are abundant from the farming experience, such as food production, animal husbandry and community development (Peter et al. 2000; Salamon et al. 1997; Stebbins 2007/2015). The unique ethos that has recently developed around small-scale sustainable farming marks commonly shared values, beliefs and attitudes in groups such as the Local Growers

Guild of southern Indiana (Fisk et al. 2000, chap. 12). All the while, small scale-sustainable farmers "identify strongly with their chosen pursuits" (Stebbins 2007/2015, 11; Stock 2007).

This last observation squares with conclusions reached in a study by Rubino et al. (2009): "Self-employed individuals pursue an activity they enjoy (that is, a hobby) as a business venture, they apparently experience feelings of reduced efficacy rather than emotional exhaustion or cynicism as they experience misfit and decreased motivation."

Conclusion

Social enterprise is missing from the foregoing discussion, mainly because there is so little research on the subject conducted from the angle of leisure studies. That said, Durieux and Stebbins (2010) have examined social enterprise from the standpoint of the SLP, using both a theoretic and an applied lens. They viewed such activity as a kind of altruism. These entrepreneurs create and implement innovative solutions to what they define as social problems, which may be local, national or international. In social entrepreneurship, people use the principles of enterprise to engender social change, done by establishing and managing a venture. Some of them set up small, medium or large non-profit groups designed to ameliorate a difficult situation threatening certain people, flora or fauna or a certain aspect of the environment, if not a combination of these. Others are profit-seekers. They hope to establish a money-making enterprise that also aims to improve a threatening situation in one of these four areas. Here devotee work becomes a possibility.

Nonetheless, empirical work is becoming more common here. Burns (2001) defines lifestyle enterprises as businesses that not only provide adequate income but also allow the owner and manager to engage in an activity that brings that person self-fulfillment. Lifestyle entrepreneurs are, therefore, people who create a new business venture that aligns with their personal values, interests and identities (Jones et al. 2020; Wright and Wiersma 2019).

Finally, note that the coverage of small devotee business in this chapter has necessarily been selective. My intention has been to present an *aperçu* of this area rather than an exhaustive survey of it. The fields of planning, product marketing and the service occupations contain an exceptionally wide variety of work activities theoretically capable of offering occupational devotion. Hopefully, I have introduced discussed a sufficient number and variety of small devotee businesses to show that, together, they constitute a fecund area of research for careers in the serious pursuits.

Notes

1   The International Association of Professional Organizations is an umbrella organization serving groups specializing in cake decorating, catering, dance studios, chocolate makers, web designers, yoga studio owners, among others. Each of these member organizations offers online short courses and certificates in their specialty.
2   The National Society of Genealogists (NSG) discusses from the standpoint of the hobbyist the ins and outs of becoming a professional genealogist, in particular looking into the skills needed to engage in the activity at this level and to conduct it as a business (https://www.ngsgenealogy.org/free-resources/becoming-a-professional-genealogist). The International Commission for Accreditation of Professional Genealogists is the credentialling body for these professionals.

Chapter 6

CONCLUSIONS

How good a living is possible by devotee work? The foregoing chapters suggest a most complex answer to this question. It roots in the observation that money has been a problem for over two centuries. Thus, Sophocles, ancient Greek priest, general and tragic poet, lamented in his drama *Antigone* that "there's nothing in the world so demoralizing as money." Accordingly, the main part of this chapter examines the bread-and-butter issue of getting paid to do devotee work. A passage from Stebbins (2004/2014, 91–100), paraphrased in the next section, sheds further light on the matter.

Are They Paid so They May Work?

Most people, lured by the opposite logic of this proposition, work so they may be paid. When work is uninteresting, but still decently remunerative, workers can at least sustain life and, with whatever money that is leftover, enjoy a bit of the smorgasbord of consumer opportunities that the commercial world lays out before them. A lifetime of uninteresting work is a high price to pay for economic survival and some spending cash, but many a modern worker finds just this bargain with that person's educational qualifications and personal standards for occupational success.

When work is highly attractive, however, this conventional orientation toward it and its remuneration often gets stood on its head. Still, the relationship of remuneration to devotee work is complicated, as is evident in the different economic situations that devotees live in or strive to live in.

Economic situation

"Economic situation" is my term for the level of living made possible by a person's disposable wealth, that being in most instances his occupational income, though in some instances, it includes returns on investments. Applied to occupational devotion, economic situation can be conceptualized as arrayed along a scale of increasing wealth that runs from poverty to opulence. The low end of the scale is anchored in *poverty* and *near poverty*, where the devotee is desperately trying to make a living, but so far with little monetary success. Here is the home of the legendary starving artist and the minimally successful small business proprietor. Here, money earned at devotee work is problematic only, though still very profoundly, in that there is little or none of it. Life is sustained by supplementary work, much of it mainly unskilled such as driving a taxi or washing dishes at a restaurant. Consider the old joke: "What do you say to the musicologist who knocks on your door one evening around dinner time?" The answer: "Thanks for the pizza, and here's a small tip."

With some financial success, struggling artists and business people are wafted up the economic situation scale toward the level of *passable living*. Here, they are joined by other kinds of occupational devotees, most of whom are just starting their chosen line of work and who have had the good fortune to avoid the poverty stage. These *arriviste* artists and others share the level of passable living with newly minted apprentice trades workers, consultants and counselors fresh from university programs who have just hung out their shingles, and the owners of recently inaugurated small businesses who, from the beginning, have managed to turn a decent profit. Passable living consists, in the main, of eating nutritious meals on a regular basis, lodging in a reasonably safe and healthy social and physical environment and having enough free time beyond work hours for adequate bodily maintenance (e.g., sleep, exercise) as well as relaxation and personal development through leisure.

With still greater monetary success, devotees enjoying a passable living may advance farther up the economic situation scale to the realm of *comfortable living*. Living comfortably builds on the base of passable living, by adding significant discretionary income with which to buy a variety of consumer goods that make life easier and more enjoyable than was possible during passable existence. This includes expanding one's personal definition of the good life to include acquisitions that go well beyond minimum standards, such as a house though an apartment would do, a BMW or Mercedes-Benz, when a Ford would do, or designer clothes when mass produced apparel would do. Although many occupational devotees during their careers eventually reach this level of economic existence, some in fact start out on it. Graduates from training programs in the most lucrative professions, among them law, medicine, engineering and computer science, offer many fine examples. That is, unless they are saddled with huge school-related debts the retirement of which might force them into passable living for several years. And it is not impossible that, once in a while, a devotee small business becomes a roaring success from the outset, as could happen with an instantly profitable restaurant or family farm (following a few good, back-to-back growing seasons).

At the top end of the economic situation scale lies *opulent living*. Devotees at these lofty heights enjoy amounts of discretionary cash far in excess of their counterparts at the next lowest level. Opulence permits conspicuous consumption. It also permits investments of various sorts, which in good economic times enable these devotees to acquire other sources of wealth in addition to the revenue they receive directly from pursuing the core activity of their occupation. This situation, we shall see shortly, also gives these devotees a certain flexibility, or margin of maneuver, when it comes to sticking to purely devotee activities or seeking extra income by working part of the time at less fulfilling, albeit decently, paying employment. Very few occupational devotees start out at this level, but some do advance this far up the economic situation scale. Most who do are in the sports and entertainment fields or, more rarely, one of the lucrative professions.

This economic situation scale is an objective tool, intended to help us understand how occupational devotees are distributed along the dimension of wealth. And, to give the scale greater precision, future empirical work in this area should include some quantitative measures of its levels of poverty, passable living and so on. Meanwhile, subjectively speaking, individual devotees may define themselves differently, which is especially likely among those living passably or comfortably near the middle of the scale. For example, some devotees, just as some non-devotees, might be inclined to argue that, even if science objectively classifies them as enjoying a comfortable living, they are in their experience just getting by on the passable level.

Orientations toward money

There are three critical orientations toward the question of pay for devotee work. One I will dub the *principled orientation*: Occupational devotees and would-be devotees seek pay for pursuing their core activity, so they can do it more often than they can as serious leisure enthusiasts. They seek to be paid so they may work. The second orientation—labeled as the *acquisitive orientation*—is that devotees and would-be devotees see their devotee occupation as offering a comfortable living, perhaps even an opulent one; that is, it is a job offering substantially greater remuneration than needed to live passably. They work so they may be paid; they see their remuneration as high enough to allow for an elevated standard living. The personal plan directing these devotees is to eventually abandon their fulfilling work for work returning substantial extrinsic rewards, thereby giving substance to Sophocles' observation. The third orientation combines the first two—call it the *principled-acquisitive orientation*; motivated by this disposition devotees seek to be paid so they may work, but at the same time, see no reason why they cannot sooner or later achieve at least a comfortable living in the bargain.

This is where occupational devotion is put to the test. At which point, if at any, do the devotees sell their occupational soul to the monetary devil? When does making more money take precedence over performing fulfilling work?

Principled devotee work

Principled devotees search for little more than the minimum needed to routinely carry out their devotee work. That is, were more money than needed for this suddenly to become available, this type would not turn it down, unless accepting it impeded in some important way pursuit of the core activity. But money is not a supreme value for these devotees. What is of supreme value is being able to routinely carry out their fulfilling work and realize in their own way the five cultural values presented by Robin Williams (2000, 146): achievement, success, freedom, activity (involvement in something) and individual personality. In the social world of the principled devotees' occupation, they would be considered insiders. Moreover, they can only be fully principled while living passably, comfortably or opulently. Devotees living in or near poverty are forced by their economic circumstances to seek money outside their core activity. They are principled part of the time but not all the time, for they must perform a modicum of remunerated, non-devotee work so they may eat and pay the rent (and have time to improve at their serious pursuit).

This way of establishing these top priorities of life is probably more easily effected in some fields than others. In the fine arts, where most devotees fall at or just above the low end of the economic situation scale, it is perhaps expedient to be principled in that there is, in any case, often little choice. This way of making virtue of necessity is likely evident as well in some small businesses, particularly artistic craftwork, restoration and repair and family farming on marginally productive soil. Still, casual observation suggests that principled devotees can be found in all four devotee areas. It is just that, in occupations such as law and medicine and because of their normally higher remuneration, most devotees start out farther up the economic situation scale on or near the level of comfortable living.

The archetypical starving artist numbers among the principled devotees. Yet, such people exist somewhere below the level of passable living. Typically, nutritious meals are not regularly at hand while lodging is substandard, in that it is neither reasonably safe nor properly located in a healthy social and physical environment. Some small business devotees find themselves in similar straits. In other words, starving artists and their equivalents in other occupations hope sooner or later to quit their Spartan life for one experienced as at least pass-able, but not if that means abandoning substantially their devotee passion.

Acquisitive devotee work

Acquisitive devotees are, as devotees, here today but gone tomorrow, having used their fulfilling activity as a springboard to vault them into work cap-able of generating significant wealth. This hope for the pecuniary good life, acquired through devotee work, is most realistic in the professions and in some of the professional consulting and counseling fields. These devotees reason that here we have interesting, prestigious, yet fulfilling work at which we can eventually make plenty of money. The acquisitive orientation is strong in this case, even if the initial attraction to the devotee occupation, which is just as strong, is substantially framed in a desire for fulfillment. Detailed research may show that, earlier in their careers, most acquisitive devotees picture themselves as principled-acquisitive devotees, rather than purely acquisitive ones.

But, when lured by opportunities for generating ever more income, the typ-ical acquisitive devotee, unlike his typical principled cousin, rarely says no. For some acquisitive devotees, these opportunities involve further remunerated pursuit of the core activity. The dilemma here is that, in their thirst for more money, they drink in more work than they can handle, which as pointed out in the preceding chapter, tends to quickly water down its fulfilling qualities. The job has now spun out of the individual's control, losing its appeal in the pro-cess. The university professor who gets into the predicament of trying to write at the same time two contracted textbooks risks falling into this trap. Writing texts can certainly be fulfilling, but that effect quickly wears off in face of too many publishers' deadlines.

Additionally, in some professional fields, opportunities arise that can charm money-oriented, acquisitive devotees away from their fulfilling work. The fine arts professions are particularly susceptible to this siren call, where it is com-monly referred to as "going commercial." Many a serious painter, novelist, jazzman and symphony musician has been unable to resist the chance to make much more money producing something that sells well to a sizeable segment of the general public. Though some acquisitive devotees manage to keep a hand in their devotee art while profiting mightily in its commercial wing, those most stirred by the appeal of opulent living tend to carry on into a full-time quest for financial success, with the initial devotee work eventually being aban-doned. Thus, jazz trumpeter Miles Davis went through his final years as a rock musician (albeit with some links to jazz), something like singer Rosemary Clooney did, who, though also initially a jazz artist, wound up singing pop until late in her career when she returned to her original passion.

Organizationally based occupational devotees must sometimes deal with their own alluring calls for greater income, which if heeded, may threaten the pursuit of their core devotee activity. As observed elsewhere for today's mid- and large-sized bureaucracies (Stebbins 2004/2014, 83–84), the few true devotee professionals employed here do sometimes get recruited to positions that remove them altogether from their devotee work. A substantially higher salary is one justification for making this career change, which may, however, come at great cost to intrinsic job fulfillment. Some devotees who make this jump may also be attracted by the prestige and perquisites that go with posts higher in the organization's structure, such as those of dean, director or vice president.

Acquisitive devotees may even turn up in the world of small business. This happens when the little enterprise becomes so successful that its owner begins to think of expanding it. There are doubtlessly many reasons for contemplating such growth, with the possibility of making considerably more money clearly being one of them. But expansion is accompanied by many new challenges that, together, will surely force the devotee entrepreneur to abandon the captivating core activity. For instance, because this person must now oversee operations in more offices than previously, there will now be little or no time for the love of repairing glass and ceramic objects or designing websites.

Construction workers who start their own enterprise in, say, plumbing, painting or plastering, can eventually meet up with similar problems. To the extent that these new businesses succeed, they will need to hire more tradespeople to carry out the core activity. This, in turn, will engender more paperwork and managerial problems, which are bound sooner or later to take the owner from the field and the core activity to the office and the world of administration.

Principled-acquisitive devotee work

Principled-acquisitive devotees not only hope to find great financial success doing fulfilling work, they also manage to achieve exactly that. Some, like the acquisitive devotees, probably start their amateur or hobbyist years inspired by this vision. Others, as they realize their own potential in their chosen field and see how it might pay off financially in the future, begin only then to, in effect, view themselves as principled-acquisitive devotees.

Highly economically successful professionals who still work as devotees have succeeded in retaining control over the flow of their fulfilling work. They have managed to become well paid for doing something that has the appeal of leisure, a rare situation indeed in modern society. Occupational devotees are uncommon enough, but those who do well financially are in even shorter supply. It is as if employers, in particular, and society, in general, know intuitively that people whose work is a passion will, other things equal, settle for substantially lower remuneration than those whose work is in some major way disagreeable. In harmony with this proposition, we have seen that many occupational devotees, like their serious leisure counterparts, regard the reward of monetary return as of secondary importance, compared with such rewards as self-enhancement, self-actualization and group accomplishment. And perhaps these devotees (both principled and principled-acquisitive) know intuitively that life is good with their present work, and that it could be a lot worse were they to take up a non-devotee occupation, even if it pays a much better salary.

This raises the question of whether occupational devotees are being exploited by their employers. Surely, some must feel this way, when they see what others are being paid who have similar qualifications and levels of experience. And in some occupations this gap may be partially reduced through collective pressure from a trade union or similar wage bargaining unit. The effect of this action, to the extent it succeeds, is to push principled devotees toward, and perhaps even into, the class of principled-acquisitive devotees. But in the university world, where the charge of exploitation is possibly most often voiced and is perhaps most valid, such collective pressure, though usually possible, is by no means always effective. Of the huge range of occupations represented in a typical North American university, the vast majority have a variety of opposite numbers in government and industry, where pay levels are generally significantly higher than in the universities. So, here, the exploitation thesis has some validity. But there is also a subtle counterargument: occupational devotees, including those in universities, already receive significant rewards for their work (i.e., those discussed in Chapters 4 and 5), rewards that many non-devotee workers wish they had. This inequity, it could be argued, is offset, at least to some extent, by giving a higher wage to the latter than to the former.

The criterion of control over the amount and disposition of time put into fulfilling work enforces a sort of upper limit on the category of principled-acquisitive devotee. There is no doubt famous and hence frequently sought out, surgeons, architects, criminal lawyers and the like who retain such control and thereby remain solid members of this category. They can refuse all but the most appealing work and hold that work to a manageable level. But what about the renowned athletes and entertainers who work for organizations that have substantial say in when and where they work?

It might appear, at first blush, that the multimillion-dollar players in football, baseball, hockey and basketball, exemplify well, if not ideally, the principled-acquisitive occupational devotee. Yet in fact, they have lost significant control over disposition of the time they spend at their calling. For with such high wages, their owners are strongly inclined to force them to play as much as possible, and to arrange for seasons filled with a slate of matches sufficient large to bring amounts of money required to offset those wages. The result is that all players, the most highly paid included, play in any one season far more of their sport than they would like. This is not, however, a question of career boredom (see Stebbins 2004/2014, 88–89). Rather, if my study of amateur and professional football players in Canada is any indication (Stebbins 1993b, 96), it is the boredom (and fatigue) that accumulates with the extended participation in practice sessions that roll on inexorably between each match. By contrast, the matches themselves were said to be exciting whenever they were scheduled during the season.

> In fact, the players in heavily commercialized sports often lose effective control over the conditions of their own sport participation. These conditions come under the control of general managers, team owners, corporate sponsors, advertisers, media personnel, marketing and publicity staff, professional management staff, accountants, and agents. The organizations that control commercial sports are intended to coordinate the interests of all these people, but their primary goal is to maximize revenues. This means that organizational decisions generally reflect the combined economic interests of many people having no direct personal connection with a sport or the athletes involved in it. The power to affect these decisions is grounded in resources that may not be connected with sports. Therefore, athletes in many commercial sports find themselves cut out of decision-making processes, even when the decisions affect their health and the rewards they receive for playing (Coakley 2001, 328).

But how about players of individual sports, who would seem to be more in control of their own work? They are, after all, not owned by a team. The top ones do have important sponsorships, however, arrangements that place significant control of their professional lives in the hands of other people. Being financially tied thus to an equipment manufacturer, for instance, creates dependence on that company. Furthermore, to realize its investments in its sponsored players, the company often tells the latter when, where and how often they will play.

In short, a good case can be made for the rich and famous in the world of sport that they are not occupational devotees at all. Instead, the purest devotees in the professional athlete class are to be found among the unsung, unsponsored journeypeople of individual sport. Their economic situation, depending on their ranking in their sport, ranges from passable to comfortable living. Meanwhile, in popular team sport, even the journeypeople lack significant control over their work, since they, too, must play through seasons the length of which is certainly not of their making (for association football, see Smith and Panja 2021).

It is much the same with top entertainers, at least for those tied to an agent (and most are). Additionally, they may have, much like highly visible, professional athletes, a personal manager, an accountant and the recurrent need to deal with media people and marketing and publicity personnel. Thus, they, too, lose their grip on their devotee attachment to their occupation, suggesting, as just done with athletes, that here, as well, the devotee in purest form is to be found primarily among the lesser and more ordinarily remunerated souls.

Well paid occupational devotees help comprise what Richard Florida (2002) describes as the "creative class." But, as is evident in this chapter, not all devotees are highly remunerated, especially those just starting out. Moreover, it is clear that creative people can be employed in situations that fail to engender devotion to their job. At fault here, often, is a social or physical milieu that is inimical to creative work or a set of organizational requirements that removes the level of control that devotee workers must have over their own time.

Teaching as a devotee support role

Teaching in the form of private lessons, adult education courses and college/university appointments are common ways of making ends meet among the occupational devotees discussed in this book. Such activity can be a devotee pursuit of its own or, as treated of here, a reasonably agreeable work role to be abandoned once acceptable full-time occupational devotion is possible. Still, full-time devotee work may not be possible, because of limited demand for the participant's product or service at a marketable price.

This situation may lead to part-time devotee work, as in weekend jazz and dance gigs, evening craft work or limited weekly opening hours for a service or sales outlet. Moreover, these workers may cycle in to and out of full- and part-time employment in their passion, as opportunities ebb and flow with the season, economy, health of the participant and the like. This aspect of the devotee career lacks research, but when it begins to accumulate, it will show further the complex relationship that can emerge between work and leisure.

The Future of Devotee Work

This book has been a timely discussion, for as I draw it to a close in mid-2021, there is talk about the nature of work post-Covid-19. Today, in many countries, many people have acquired a taste for working at home and the freedom it brings vis-à-vis commuting daily to the office, plant or store and the rigidity and boredom of their job and associated activities. No surprise, perhaps.

Working from home, even if only for part of the work week, may help meet two of the six criteria for occupational devotion, namely, having control over the amount and disposition of time put into the job and working in a physical and social milieu that encourages devotee activity. I am not saying here that work at home is necessarily devotee in nature, since in fact, most of it is not. It is only that such change in the daily grind is often welcome because it meets both criteria.

Neil Irwin (2021) has argued that today

> employers are becoming much more cognizant that yes, it's about money, but also about quality of life […]. [Whether] it's a bigger pay-check, more manageable hours or a training opportunity offered to a person with few formal credentials, the benefits of a tight labor market and shifting leverage can take many forms.

Highly attractive work can sometimes emerge from this occupational ferment, though historically, it seems uncommon. Finding work that is serious leisure from which a living is possible is more common, even if it is hardly a dom-inant arrangement in the modern era. Nevertheless, that many employees and some employers are now focusing more than usually on the quality of work life is a sign that this part of our existence may at last be up for a badly needed improvement.

REFERENCES

Ackley, D. (2019). Is homebrewing art or science? https://blog.eckraus.com/is-homebrewing-art-or-science, retrieved November 29, 2020.

Alonso, A. D., Alexander, N., and O'Brien, S. (2017). "Every brew is a challenge and every glass of a good beer is an achievement": Home brewing and serious leisure. *Leisure/Loisir*, 42(1), 93–113, doi: 10.1080/14927713.2017.1414628.

Arenas, A. (2008). Connecting hand, mind, and community: Vocational education for social and environmental renewal. *Teachers College Record*, 110(2), 377–404.

Atkinson, M. M. (2003). *Tattooed: The sociogenesis of a body art*. Toronto: University of Toronto Press.

Baldwin, C. K., and Norris, P. A. (1999). Exploring the dimensions of serious leisure: Love me—love my dog. *Journal of Leisure Research*, 31, 1–17.

Barbour, R. (2020). Calligraphy. *Encyclopedia Britannica*, online edition, retrieved December 9, 2020.

Becker, H. S. (1982). *Art worlds*. Berkeley, CA: University of California Press.

Bluespan (2016). The rise of the internet amateur meteorology, June 30. https://bluespan.com/blog/the-rise-of-the-internet-amateur-meteorology, retrieved March 22, 2021.

Brayham, A. (2015). Never stop improving: The complexity and contradictions of DIY home renovating as a serious leisure pursuit. *Loisir et Société/Society and Leisure*, 38(1), 88–99, doi: 10.1080/07053436.2015.1006962.

Brett-MacLean, P. J. (2007). Art(ists) in the making: Exploring narratives of coming to art in later life. Doctoral dissertation, Faculty of Graduate Studies, University of British Columbia (Canada).

Brown, P. L. (2020). Gone but never forgotten in a quilt. *New York Times*, December 17, online edition.

Bryan, H. (1977). Leisure value systems and recreational specialization: The case of trout fishermen. *Journal of Leisure Research*, 9, 174–87.

Bureau of Labor Statistics, U.S. Department of Labor (2020). *Occupational outlook handbook*, Craft and Fine Artists, at https://www.bls.gov/ooh/arts-and-design/craft-and-fine-artists.htm, visited December 20, 2020.

Burns, P. (2001). *Entrepreneurship and Small Business*. Tavistock and Rochdale: Palgrave Macmillan.

Case, D. O. (2009). Serial collecting as leisure, and coin collecting in particular. *Library Trends*, 57, 729–52.

Chevalier, V., Le Manq, F., and Simonet, M. (2011). Amateurs, bénévoles et professionnelles: Analyse des carrières et usages des statuts. In A. Degenne, C. Marry, and S. Moulin (eds.), *Les catégories sociales et leurs frontières* (pp. 147–64). Québec, QC: Les Presses de l'Université Laval.

Coakley, J. (2001). *Sport in society: Issues and controversies*, 7th ed. New York: McGraw-Hill.

Cooper, E. (2000). *Ten thousand years of pottery*. London: British Museum Press.

Craig, A. (2007). Practicing poetry: A career without a job. In C. Calhoun and R. Sennett (eds.), *Practicing culture (taking culture seriously)* (pp. 35–56). New York: Routledge

Dashper, K., Abbott, J., and Wallace, C. (2020). 'Do horses cause divorces?' Autoethnographic insights on family, relationships and resource-intensive leisure. *Annals of Leisure Research*, 23(3), 304–21, doi: 10.1080/11745398.2019.1616573.

Davidson, L., and Stebbins, R. A. (2011). *Serious leisure and nature: Sustainable consumption in the outdoors*. Basingstoke: Palgrave Macmillan.

de Lauwere, C. C., Drost, H., de Buck, A. J., Smit, A. B., Balk-Theuws, L. W., Buurma, J. S., and Prins, H. (2004). To change or not to change? Farmers' motives to convert to integrated or organic farming (or not). Retrieved from http://www.actahort.org.

Durieux, M. B., and Stebbins, R. A. (2010). *Social entrepreneurship for dummies*. Hoboken, NJ: Wiley.

Farmer, J. (2012). Leisure in living local through food and farming. *Leisure Sciences*, 34, 490–95.

Fine, G. A. (1998). *Morel tales: The culture of mushrooming*. Cambridge, MA: Harvard University Press.

Fisher, Max (2012). *What makes America's gun culture totally unique in the world, in four charts*. *Washington Post*, December 15, retrieved December 8, 2020.

Fisk, J. W., Hersterman, O. B., and Thorburn, T. L. (2000). Integrated farming systems: A sustainable agriculture learning community in the USA. In N. G. Röling and M. A. E. Wagemakers (eds.), *Facilitating sustainable agriculture: Participatory learning and adaptive management in time of environmental uncertainty* (pp. 217–31). Cambridge, England: Cambridge University Press.

Florida, R. (2002). *The rise of the creative class and how it's transforming work, leisure, community and everyday life*. New York: Basic Books.

Gillespie, D. L., Leffler, A., and Lerner, E. (2002). If it weren't my hobby, I'd have a life: Dog sports, serious leisure, and boundary negotiations. *Leisure Studies, 21*, 285–304.

Gould, J., Moore, D., McGuire, F., and Stebbins, R. A. (2008). Development of the serious leisure inventory and measure. *Journal of Leisure Research*, 40(1), 47–68.

Gunsmith (2020). In *Wikipedia, The Free Encyclopedia*. Retrieved 16:48, December 8, 2020, from https://en.wikipedia.org/w/index.php?title=Gunsmith&oldid=961807681.

Habenstein, R.W. (1992). Sociology of occupations: The case of the American funeral director. In A.M. Rose (ed.), *Human behavior and social processes* (pp. 225–46). Boston, MA: Houghton Mifflin.

Hackley, C., and Kover, A. (2007). The trouble with creatives: Negotiating creative identity in advertising agencies, *International Journal of Advertising* 26(1), 63–78.

Hartel, J. (2003). The serious leisure frontier in library and information science: Hobby domains. *Knowledge Organization*, 30(3/4), 228–38.

———. (2007). Information activities, resources, and spaces in the hobby of gourmet cooking. Doctoral dissertation, Los Angeles, CA: University of California.

Henderson, S., and Spracklen, K. (2014). From serious leisure to serious work, or, when folk music struck a chord: Habermasian rationality and agency. *Leisure/Loisir*, 38, 207–24.

Hershkovitz, A., and Hardof-Jaffe, S. (2017). Genealogy as a lifelong endeavor. *Leisure/Loisir*, 41(4), 535–60.

Hilbert, J. R. (1994). *Home handyman: An exploratory study*. Master's thesis, Department of Sociology, University of Calgary (Canada).

Hultsman, W. (2015). Dogs and companion/performance sport: Unique social worlds, serious leisure enthusiasts, and solid human-canine partnerships. In N. Carr (ed.), *Domestic animals and leisure* (pp. 35–66). Houndmills: Palgrave Macmillan.

Irwin, N. (2021). Workers are gaining leverage over employers right before our eyes. *New York Times,* June 5, online edition.

Jackson, Ann. (2020). Women studio furniture makers: A longitudinal study. Retrieved from the University of Minnesota Digital Conservancy, Acta Horticulturae | International Society for Horticultural Science (ishs.org).

Jones, P., Ratten, V., and Hayduk, T. (2020). Sport, fitness, and lifestyle entrepreneurship. *International Entrepreneurship and Management Journal*, 16, 783–93, doi: 10.1007/s11365-020-00666-x.

Jourdain A., and Naulin S. (2020). Making money out of leisure: The marketization of handicrafts and food blogging. In S. Naulin and A. Jourdain (eds.), *The social meaning of extra money. Dynamics of virtual work* (pp. 61–95). Cham: Palgrave Macmillan, https://doi.org/10.1007/978-3-030-18297-7_3.

Juniu, S., Tedrick, T., and Boyd, R. (1996). Leisure or work? Amateur and professional musicians' perception of rehearsal and performance. *Journal of Leisure Research*, 28, 44–56.

King, F. L. (2001). Social dynamics of quilting. *World Leisure Journal*, 43(2), 26–29.

Kuusi, T., and Haukola, P. (2017). Double life. Music as work and serious leisure. *Journal of Arts and Humanities*, 6(3), 18–32.

Le Fur, E. (2021). Collectors' motives in the context of wealth management. *Journal of Asset Management*, published online, doi.org/10.1057/s41260-021-00221-5.

Lim, S. M., and Lee, K. M. (2013). The relationship among achievement goal orientation, passion with serious leisure in tennis club members. *Korean Journal of Physical Education*, 52(1), 101–15.

MacCosham, B., and Gravelle, F. (2017). Leisure lifestyle's influence on serious leisure: A look at dropout amateur Junior ice hockey players. *Loisir et Société/Society and Leisure*, 40(2), 213–27.

McQuarrie, F., and Jackson, E. L. (1996). Connections between negotiation of leisure constraints and serious leisure: An exploratory study of adult amateur ice skaters. *Loisir et Société/Society and Leisure*, 19, 459–83.

Mara, A. (2020). The armchair detectives using the web to catch criminals: True crime series, podcasts and genealogy databases are inspiring amateur detectives. *The Irish Times*, February 4, online edition. https://www.irishtimes.com/culture/books/the-armchair-detectives-using-the-web-to-catch-criminals-1.4160445, retrieved May 27, 2021.

Marnin-Distelfeld, S. (2020). Serious leisure visual artists in Israel: Challenging amateurism. *International Journal of Sociology of Leisure*, 3, 311–28, https://doi.org/10.1007/s41978-020-00063-2.

Mellor, B. E. (2006). Radical shift: A grounded theory approach to midlife career change of professionals. Master's thesis, Department of Sociology, University of Calgary.

Morris, C., and Endfield, G. (2012). Exploring contemporary amateur meteorology through an historical lens. *Weather*, 67(1), 4–8.

Muir, D. E. (1991). Club tennis: A case study in taking leisure very seriously. *Sociology of Sport Journal*, 8(1), 70–78, doi: 10.1123/ssj.8.1.70.

Nardi, P. M. (1984). Toward a social psychology of entertainment magic (conjuring). *Symbolic Interaction*, 7(1), 25–42, https://doi.org/10.1525/si.1984.7.1.25.

National Quilter's Circle (2020). Glossary of quilting terms and definitions. https://www.nationalquilterscircle.com/article/glossary-of-quilting-terms/#, retrieved December 14, 2020.

Olmsted, A. D. (1991). Collecting: Leisure, investment, or obsession? *Journal of Social Behavior and Personality*, 6, 287–306.

Orchiston, W. (2014). The amateur-turned professional syndrome: Two Australian case studies. In W. Orchiston, D. A. Green, and R. Strom (eds.), *New insights from recent studies in historical astronomy: Following in the footsteps of F. Richard Stephenson* (pp. 259–350). New York: Springer.

Peter, G., Mayerfeld-Bell, M., Jarnagain, S., and Bauer, D. (2000). Coming back across the fence: Masculinity and transition to sustainable agriculture. *Rural Sociology*, 65(2), 215–33.

Piskunova, I. (2010). Amateurism in Saratov local history research. In M. Stuart-Hoyle and J. Lovell (eds.), *Leisure experiences: Space, place and performance*, LSA No. 109 (pp. 113–42). Eastbourne: Chelsea School, University of Brighton.

Poór, J., and Józsa, I. (2015). The evolution of the external consultant involvement in human resource management in eastern Europe. *Journal of Eastern European and Central Asian Research*, 2(1), 1–9, http://dx.doi.org/10.15549/jeecar.v2i1.70.

Ramirez, M. (2019). *Destined for greatness: Passions, dreams, and aspirations in a college music town*. New Brunswick, NJ: Rutgers University Press.

Ribeiro, N. F. (2017). Boxing culture and serious leisure among North American youth: An embodied ethnography. *The Qualitative Report*, 22(6), 1622–36, https://doi.org/10.46743/2160-3715/2017.2715.

Rubino, C., Luksyte, A., Perry, S. J., and Volpone, S. D. (2009). How do stressors lead to burnout? The mediating role of motivation. *Journal of Occupational Health Psychology*, 14(3), 289–304.

Salamon, S., Farnsworth, R., Bullock, D., and Yusuf, R. (1997). Family factors affecting the adoption of sustainable farming practices. *Journal of Soil and Water Conservation*, 52(4), 265–71.

Schell, B. H., and Zinger, J. T. (1985). An investigation of self-actualization, job satisfaction, and job commitment for Ontario funeral directors. *Psychological Reports*, 57(2),455–64, doi: 10.2466/pr0.1985.57.2.455.

Schupp, K. (2020). I can't, I have dance: Dance competition culture as serious leisure and pre-professional training. *Leisure Studies*, 39(4), 479–92, doi: 10.1080/02614367.2019.1643902.

Scott, D., and McMahan, K. K. (2017). Hard-core leisure: Conceptualizations. *Leisure Sciences*, 39(6), 569–74.

Siegenthaler, K. L., and O'Dell, I. (2003). Older golfers: Serious leisure and successful aging. *World Leisure Journal*, 45(1), 45–52.

Smith, R., and Panja, T. (2021). A soccer summer's common opponent: Fatigue. *New York Times*, June 9, online edition.

Stalp, M. C. (2006). Creating an artistic self: Amateur quilters and subjective careers. *Sociological Focus*, 39, 193–216.

———, M. C. (2007). *Quilting: The fabric of everyday life*. New York: Berg.

Stalp, M. C., and Conti, R. (2011). Serious leisure in the home: Professional quilters negotiate family space. *Gender, Work and Organization*, 18, 399–414.

Stebbins, R. A. (1976). Music among friends: The social networks of amateur musicians. *International Review of Sociology* (Series II), 12, 52–73.

————, R. A. (1979). *Amateurs: On the margin between work and leisure.* Beverly Hills, CA: Sage Publications (digital copy available at www.seriousleisure.net).

————, R. A. (1980). Avocational science: The amateur routine in archaeology and astronomy. *International Journal of Comparative Sociology,* 21 (March–June), 34–48.

————, R. A. (1982a). Serious leisure: A conceptual statement. *Pacific Sociological Review,* 25, 251–72.

————, R. A. (1982b). Amateur and professional astronomers: A study of their interrelationships. *Urban Life,* 10, 433–54.

————, R. A. (1990). *The laugh-makers: Stand-up comedy as art, business, and life-style.* Montréal, QC and Kingston, ON: McGill-Queen's University Press.

————, R. A. (1992). *Amateurs, professionals, and serious leisure.* Montreal, QC and Kingston, ON: McGill-Queen's University Press.

————, R. A. (1993a). *Career, culture and social psychology in a variety art: The magician.* Malabar, FL: Krieger (reprinted edition with Introduction). Original edition published in 1984 as *The magician: Career, culture, and social psychology in a variety art.* Toronto, ON: Irwin.

————, R. A. (1993b). *Canadian football. A view from the helmet* (reprinted ed.). Toronto, ON: Canadian Scholars Press.

————, R. A. (1994). The liberal arts hobbies: A neglected subtype of serious leisure. *Loisir et Société / Society and Leisure,* 16, 173–86.

————, R. A. (1996). Volunteering: A serious leisure perspective. *Nonprofit and Voluntary Sector Quarterly,* 25, 211–24.

————, R. A. (2002). *The organizational basis of leisure participation: A motivational exploration.* State College, PA: Venture.

————, R. A. (2004a). Fun, enjoyable, satisfying, fulfilling: Describing positive leisure experience. *Leisure Studies Association Newsletter,* 69 (November), 8–11 (also freely available at www.seriousleisure.net—Digital Library).

————, R. A. (2004b). Pleasurable aerobic activity: A type of casual leisure with salubrious implications. *World Leisure Journal,* 46(4), 55–58.

————, R. A. (2004c). Stamp collecting. In G. S. Cross (ed.), *Encyclopedia of recreation and leisure in America* (pp. 310–11). New York: Charles Scribner's Sons.

————, R. A. (2004/2014). *Between work and leisure: The common ground of two separate worlds.* New Brunswick, NJ: Transaction/New York: Routledge, 2017 (paperback edition with new Preface, 2014).

————, R. A. (2005a). *Challenging mountain nature: Risk, motive, and lifestyle in three hobbyist sports.* Calgary, AB: Detselig.

————, R. A. (2005b). Project-based leisure: Theoretical neglect of a common use of free time. *Leisure Studies,* 24, 1–11.

————, R. A. (2006). Mentoring as a leisure activity: On the informal world of small-scale altruism. *World Leisure Journal,* 48(4), 3–10.

————, R. A. (2007). The sociology of entertainment. In C. D. Bryant and D. L. Peck (eds.), *21st century sociology: A reference handbook,* vol. 2 (pp. 178–85).Thousand Oaks, CA: Sage.

————, R. A. (2007/2015). *Serious leisure: A perspective for our time.* New Brunswick, NJ: Transaction/New York: Routledge (2017). Published in paperback in 2015 with new Preface.

————, R. A. (2012). *The idea of leisure: First principles,* New Brunswick, NJ: Transaction/New York: Routledge (2017).

————, R. A. (2014). *Careers in serious leisure: From dabbler to devotee in search of fulfillment.* Basingstoke: Palgrave Macmillan.

————, R. A. (2015). *Leisure and the motive to volunteer: Theories of serious, casual, and project-based leisure*. Basingstoke: Palgrave Macmillan.

————, R. A. (2019). Democracy's politicians: An occupation like no other. *Society*, 56(5), 461–62, doi: 10.1007/s12115-019-00399-w.

————, R. A. (2020). *The serious leisure perspective: A synthesis*. Basingstoke: Palgrave Macmillan.

————, R. A. (2021). *Non-work obligations: On the delicate art of dealing with disagreeableness*. Bingley: Emerald Group Publishing.

Stevens-Ratchford, R. G. (2016). Ballroom dance: Linking serious leisure to successful aging. *International Journal of Aging and Human Development*, 83(3), 290–308.

Stiénon, V. (2008). Des « univers de consolation ». Note sur la sociologie des écrivains amateurs. *COnTEXTES*, hors dossier, notes de lecture, septembre 12.

Stock, P. (2007). "Good farmers" as reflexive producers: an examination of family organic farmers in the U.S. Midwest. *Sociologia Ruralis*, 47(2), 83–102.

Stone, E. (2019). What's in it for the cats? Cat shows as serious leisure from a multispecies perspective. *Leisure Studies*, 38(3), 381–93, doi: 10.1080/02614367.2019.1572776.

Study.Com (2020). Become a calligrapher: Training and career information. https://study.com/articles/Become_a_Calligrapher_Training_and_Career_Information.html, retrieved December 9, 2020.

Taylor, B. (1995). Amateurs, professionals, and the knowledge of archaeology. *British Journal of Sociology*, 46, 499–508.

Thompson Island Brewing Company (2019). What's the difference between a craft brewery, microbrewery, brewpub & gastropub? (https://thompsonislandbrewing.com/blog/whats-the-difference-between-a-craft-brewery-microbrewery-brewpub-amp-gastropub, retrieved December 26, 2020).

Thurnell-Read, T. (2016). Real ale enthusiasts, serious leisure and the costs of getting "too serious" about beer. *Leisure Sciences*, 38(1), 68–84, doi: 10.1080/01490400.2015.1046618.

Tsaur, S-H., and Liang, T-W. (2008). Serious leisure and recreation specialization. *Leisure Sciences*, 30 (2008): 325–41.

Turner, G., and McAlpine, L. (2011). Doctoral experience as researcher preparation: Activities, passion, status. *International Journal for Researcher Development*, 2(1), 46–60, https://doi.org/10.1108/17597511111178014.

Unruh, D. R. (1979). Characteristics and types of participation in social worlds. *Symbolic Interaction*, 2, 115–30.

Unruh, D. R. (1980). The nature of social worlds. *Pacific Sociological Review*, 23, 271–96.

Watling, R. (1998). The role of the amateur in mycology—What would we do without them! *Mycoscience* 39, 513–22, https://doi.org/10.1007/BF02460913.

Williams, R. M., Jr. (2000). American society. In E. F. Borgatta and R. J. V. Montgomery (eds.), *Encyclopedia of sociology*, 2nd ed., vol. 1 (pp. 140–48). New York: Macmillan.

Wilson, K. (1995). Olympians or lemmings? The postmodernist fun run. *Leisure Studies*, 14, 174–85.

Wright, R. K., and Wiersma, C. (2019). "It pays to play": The emergence of innovative planning, occupational devotion, and lifestyle entrepreneurship in Aotearoa/New Zealand. In V. Ratten (ed.), *Social entrepreneurship and public policy* (pp. 23–39). New York: Springer.

Yang, Y. (2021). Smartphone photography and its socio-economic life in China: An ethnographic analysis. *Global Media and China*, 20 (June 14), https://doi.org/10.1177/205943 64211022605.

Yoder, D. G. (1997). A model for commodity intensive serious leisure. *Journal of Leisure Research*, 29, 407–29.

INDEX

consultants 31–44
    consultant pharmacist 34–36
    consulting psychology 33–34
    education consultant 36–37
    human resources consultant 37–39
    information technology consultant 39–40
    legal nurse consultant 32–33
    media consultant 40
    political consultant 40–41
    professional engineering consultant 41–42
    theater consultant 42–43
    urban planning consultant 43–44

economic situation 69–71

future of devotee work 77–78

liberal professions 15–29

orientations toward money 71–77
    acquisitive devotee work 73–74
    principled devotee work 71–73
    principled-acquisitive devotee work 74–77

preprofessional amateurs 18–19, 27, 28, 34, 35, 37, 39–40, 42, 44, 55, 56, 60–61, 62
public-centered professions 15–17
    in the arts 17–21
    client-centered professions 28
    in entertainment 26–27
    in science 21–23
    in sport 23–26

serious leisure perspective 1–13
    career (leisure to work) 7
    casual leisure 11–12
    devotee work 5–7, 12; *See also* Chapters 2–5
    project-based leisure 12
    qualities (six) of serious pursuits 7–9
    rewards and costs of serious pursuits 9–11
    serious pursuits 2–11

skilled trades and crafts 45–57
    brewers and microbrewing 47–48
    calligraphy 52
    ceramic art 54–55
    electricians and plumbers 46–47
    floral designer 55–56
    furniture making 52–53
    gunsmithing 51
    hobbyist cooks 49
    masonry workers 45–46
    metalworkers 49–51
    plumbers 47
    quilting 54
SLP Involvement Scale 16f2.1
small businesses 59–67
    animal work 61
    artistic crafts 64
    custom work (tailors, tattooists, hair stylists, makeup artists, furniture makers, etc.) 60–61
    dealer in collectibles 61
    family farm 66–67
    planning 65–66
    product marketing 64–65
    repair and restoration 61–62
    service occupations 62–64
    skilled crafts 59
    teaching as a small business 59–60
social enterprise 67
Stebbins, R. A. 1–12

teaching as a devotee support role 77
typological structure of the SLP 3f1.1
typology of Volunteers and Volunteering 4t1.1

Unruh, D. R. 8–9

Yoder, D. G. 2

www.ingramcontent.com/pod-product-compliance
Lightning Source LLC
Chambersburg PA
CBHW031447280326
41927CB00037B/382